Friday's Winners

Putt Riddle

Friday's Winners

Putt Riddle

Copyright © 2014 Putt Riddle
All rights, reserved

ISBN: 150085672X
ISBN 13: 9781500856724

APPRECIATION TO THOSE WHO HELPED ME PREPARE *FRIDAY'S WINNERS* FOR PUBLICATION

I thank the following people who helped me or encouraged me in preparing *Friday's Winners* for publication.
Skeeter Commiskey and Kathy Siebel for proof-reading and suggesting changes to the text.
My son Brent Riddle who provided the computer skills I lacked at times.
Mary Commiskey who kept me encouraged that *Friday's Winners* was a great read even for a non-football fan.
Chris Schmidt of the UIL who provided me plenty of material from the archives of the UIL to aid me in my research.
Joe Lee Smith, the ultimate source to help me get the facts right.

TABLE OF CONTENTS

FORWARD	ix
ABOUT FRIDAY'S *WINNERS*	xi
FOOTBALL, A FAMILY TRADITION	1
RECOGNITION	8
THE AMARILLO SANDIES	14
THE BROWNWOOD LIONS	33
THE CAMERON YOE YOEMEN	42
THE CORSICANA TIGERS	50
THE CUERO GOBBLERS	58
THE HIGHLAND PARK SCOTS	67
THE HONDO OWLS	81
THE LONGVIEW LOBOS	90
THE MART PANTHERS	98
THE PLANO WILDCATS	109
THE TEMPLE WILDCATS	122
THE TYLER JOHN TYLER LIONS	135
WHEN PATHS CROSSED	144
SCORING BIG, DOMINATING ON DEFENSE	149
STREAKS AND RECORDS-TEAM & INDIVIDUAL	153
CHANGES, BUT NO SURPRISES	161
UPDATE ON 2014 GAMES	163

FORWARD

Friday's Winners is a compilation of information about the 12 winningest high school football teams in Texas.

It took me over 30 months to gather this information. I interviewed a lot of current coaches, former coaches and former players as well as dedicated fans and others in the communities I traveled to in putting this book together.

It has been a great experience meeting people all over the state who share one thing in common, their passion and love for their local high school football team. Meeting with and interviewing some of the players and coaches who previously have only been known to me as legends for their accomplishments on the gridiron has been a great trip.

Introducing myself to new people by saying that I was researching a book about the 12 high school football teams in Texas with the most wins has been a great way to get conversations started as those I was meeting wanted to share their ideas of which teams belonged in that group. It got to be funny when so many names of other schools not in this group were presented by fans who just knew that their choices belonged. Naming off those schools in *Friday's Winners* in alphabetical order many times brought out comments such as, "I had no idea." Or "I don't see how they made it." It seemed that the further away the guessers lived from the teams making the book, the less likely they were to have known just how great these 12 teams have been, are and will be in the future.

In putting together the chapters on each team, I did focus for the most part on years and decades when they were enjoying their best successes. But not always. You will also notice that I skipped decades in some cases to get a touch of what made the football programs unique at each school. I also tried to get a variety of players and coaches from different eras of their program to describe what it was like for them personally. The result is that there are stories in *Friday's Winners* from players and coaches given to me personally by them that cover 80 years of Texas high school football, not quite the 100+ year histories that most of them have in playing the game on Friday nights and other times, but close. It does leave room for the stories and detailed histories of the years not mentioned here to be told in the future for someone wanting to get those stories recorded. But I feel that when you finish reading *Fridays' Winners,* you will have learned about some unique football teams, their coaches, players, fans and traditions that make each of them feel that they are the best in the state. Their winning records show you can't argue with their success on the football field. They are all in the top 1% of the winningest teams in Texas suiting up every Friday night in the late summer into the late fall, hopefully on into the mid November to mid December playoffs to see how much they can add to their records and keep other teams from taking their places at the top. Enjoy reading about them.

ABOUT FRIDAY'S *WINNERS*

Friday's Winners is a labor of love about the Texas high schools that have won the most football games in all of Texas high school history. It came about because my alma mater is among the dozen high schools whose teams have won at least 666 games since they first suited up through 2013, in some cases for over a hundred years. Amarillo High School is my alma mater. It has been a source of pride to me that ever since I first became aware of this particular statistic, the Golden Sandies have either been the top team in total football victories in Texas or no worse than the third-ranked team. When I first learned of this mark of distinction that separates this cream from the rest of the crop, the Temple Wildcats were the top team in total wins, thanks to their remarkable run in the 1990s that included a state championship in 1992. Amarillo was a few wins back at that point.

Thanks to the constant churn 'em out win record of Larry Dippel, the Sandies head coach for 31 years, Amarillo caught and surpassed Temple even though the Sandies never played for a state championship during that run. The Amarillo supremacy lasted until 2008 when the current leader, Highland Park finally caught and passed it. Briefly, another DFW Metroplex based school, Plano Senior High, also passed the Sandies and took over second place for a few games. The Scots, led by Coach Randy Allen, have put distance between them and the few contenders for top bragging rights ever since. At this point, heading into the 2014 season, they have won 767 games. Amarillo, who fought its way back into second, aided by a downturn in the fortunes of the other schools for a season or two, is a distant second to Highland Park with 743 wins.

I began gathering my information to write *Friday's Winners* in March, 2012. At that point, there were 11 schools that stood out over the 1000 Texas high schools that are members of the University Interscholastic League playing 11 man football in total gridiron victories. There was enough distance between the two of the 11 that had the fewest number of wins at that point, 645, and the rest of the UIL members. Clearly this was the cream of the crop to focus in my book. But as the fortunes of football teams change from season to season and sometimes they're up and sometimes down for a prolonged spell, another team has won its way into the realm of the top teams in Texas. That is the Cameron Yoe Yoemen who won 30 of 31 games they played in 2012 and 2013 along with two Class 2A-DI state championships in a row. They came kicking and screaming to earn a place in *Friday's Winners.* In my book listed with their total wins are the Highland Park Scots (767), Amarillo Golden Sandstorm (743), Plano Senior High Wildcats (734), Temple Wildcats (710), Brownwood Lions (702), Mart Panthers (701), Corsicana Tigers (679), Tyler John Tyler Lions (671), Cuero Gobblers (670), Longview Lobos (668), Cameron Yoe Yoemen (667) and the Hondo Owls (666). The closest contenders to this group for inclusion are eight to 15 wins back. They include Refugio (658), Lufkin (657), Abilene (656), Garland and Wichita Falls (651 wins each).

There is a lot of research that takes place to put together a book like this, particularly when 11 of the 12 schools have game histories going back at least 100 years. It's been fun compiling that research, visiting the schools, meeting coaches and current and old players as well as some die-hard fans. Some of them have put together lots of information about their schools that they have been willing to share with me. That includes Butch Walker of Mart, Mike Weber of Cuero, Soapy Sudbury of Amarilllo, Jenni Scoggin of the Highland Park Alumni Association and Bertie Shumate of Cameron Yoe. Sadly, Weber died of a stroke on June 9th, 2014 just six days after I went to Cuero to meet him in person and see the Cuero Gobbler Football Museum which he played a key role in creating. There was no doubting his passion for Gobbler football once we began communicating two years ago. As the DeWitt County Sheriff Jode Zavesky says, "Mike was Mr Cuero Football." He will be missed by all who knew him in Cuero.

However, the person who has provided the most help on researching these schools as well as all the other high school football teams in Texas history is Joe Lee Smith. I first began talking to him when someone told me he was the most knowledgable person on the subject. He has spent 50 plus years looking up the scores of every game played by every 11 man team in Texas, taking down team and individual stats and compiling enough data about all these teams, coaches, players, records and etc that he has generously shared with many people and institutions. The records maintained by the UIL came from him. Two years ago, he made his massive data base available for anyone needing to research teams. I have heard and read of tributes of gratitude to Joe Lee for his unselfish action from people such as Smoaky (David Smoak) at ESPN1660 in Waco and Dave Campbell of the Bryan Eagle. Smoaky has his own collection of historical East Texas high school information. He says that Joe Lee made it possible for him to compile what he has.

Personally, Joe Lee has been more than generous to me providing information for this book as well as having a web site that I have liberally used to add to my personal visits to and interviews for my dynamic dozen school s. About the website, if it doesn't say it all, then it hasn't happened yet. But Joe Lee modestly disagrees with that assessment saying that there are always errors to be found, new facts to enter and a need for constant research to make sure he's got it right. So he can be found nearly every day in his East Texas lake home in his designated man cave plugging away for a few hours to make it right.

Therefore to say thanks to him for all he has done for Texas high school football, which BTW has him enshrined in the Texas High School Football Hall of Fame inside the Texas Sports Hall of Fame in Waco, I am dedicating this book to Joe Lee Smith, the most deserving man in Texas for making the records straight about the glorious game that is Texas high school football.

FOOTBALL, A FAMILY TRADITION

It didn't occur to me how playing for the same team as your dad and grand dad played would be a source of pride for players for the twelve schools in this book, That is, until I met Justin Read in his family grocery store in downtown Mart in the spring of 2012. He was on the 1999 Panther team that went 15-0 and won the AA State championship. Talk about tradition, he was working in the store that his great grandfather had opened in 1925. The fourth generation of his family to serve the Mart community in the same location. When I told him that my project was writing this book, he very quickly mentioned that his dad, Jim, had played on the 1969 Panther team that went 15-0 and won the AA State championship. What's more, his grandfather, J.B.Read, had played on the 1946 team that went 11-0 and won the Regional championship. That was as far as the Panthers could advance then. His enthusiasm for his family involvement in Mart football struck a chord with me. As long as most of these twelve schools have played, most of them already past the one hundred year mark since they first fielded a team, I thought there might be a number of families who had at least three generations of football players for their schools, perhaps even four or five generations.

So I added an amendment to my questionnaire to get that information and create this chapter. Sure enough, the response has been good and pride in the families of this accomplishment is very obvious as I interviewed those whose names were sent to me. After the Reads, I had several names of Highland Park families submitted to me by Jenni Scoggin, the Scots' alumni director. The first person I talked to was Syd Carter, a quarterback-halfback on the 1953 Scots, graduate of the class of 1954. Today he is the executive director of the Highland Park High School Foundation. He tries to raise money to offset the 75 per cent of the school district's tax revenues that are shuffled off to Austin since Highland Park is labeled as a Robin Hood school. And I thought it was bad that 54 per cent of the taxes generated by the Groesbeck ISD, mainly because of the power plant in the district, also automatically goes to Austin under the same Robin Hood label.

Syd's son, Dodge Carter was a punter for the Scots before he graduated in 1982. Dodge's son, J. Dodge Carter, filled the gap at linebacker before graduating in 2009. Syd has two daughters who gave him three additional grandsons, all of whom have worn the plaid for the Scots. John Ellerman was a quarterback on the 2005 state champion team and the 2006 team and graduated in 2007. John's younger brother, Scott Ellerman, also played quarterback before graduating in 2012. Carter Dunlap played alongside John Ellerman on the 2005 team. The defensive end graduated in 2006.

Another Scot family playing over three generations is the Sides family. Jack Davis Sides Jr., was a running back and defensive back in 1955 and 1956. His son, Jack Davis Sides II, was a fullback/running back and outside linebacker in 1985, 1986 and 1987. In 2016, the third generation, Jack Evans Sides will graduate from Highland Park. As a sophomore, he played offensive guard in 2013. He is slated to play left tackle and defensive end in 2014 and possibly in 2015.

Ed Bernet graduated from Highland Park in 1951. He was a two way player at offensive and defensive end in 1949 and 1950. In 1950, he was chosen by the Texas Sports Writers Association as the Outstanding Texas High School Player of the Year. He played for SMU in college and professionally in the NFL for Pittsburgh and in the AFL for the Dallas Texans. His sons, Blake Bernet and Brant Bernet, played for the Scots in the early 1980s. Blake was a center and linebacker for the 1980 and 1981 Scots. Brant played tight end in 1981 and 1982. Brant's two sons finished in the last five years. Chap Bernet was a left tackle on the 2008 team. Charlie Bernet was a wide receiver on the 2010 Scots.

Out in Hondo, there is one family that has had its family members play for the Owls spread out over one hundred years in a unique way. The Owls began their play in 1912. The grand father-in-law of John Zerr, Edgar Stiegler, played lineman for the first Owl team. John Zerr played linebacker and offensive guard during the 1958-61 seasons. His son and Stiegler's great grandson, Marc Zerr, was an Owl tight end during the 1982-84 years. Exactly one hundred and one years after Stieger played on that 1912 team, his great-great grandson and John Zerr's grandson, Jake Zerr was a split receiver and defensive back for both the 2011 and 2012 Owls. Another fourth generation player who will graduate in 2015 from Hondo High is the O line-D-line two way player, Max Bales, the grandson of Zerr and great-great grandson of Stiegler.

Another family in Hondo with four generations of Owl players is the Graff family. Robert Joe Graff was on the 1918 and 1919 Owl teams. His son, Robert, played in 1948 and 1949. Thirty years later in 1978 and 1979, Tom Graff played offensive tackle for Hondo. His son, Reed was a defensive tackle on the 2013 team.

There is at least one three-generation family in Hondo: Glenn McWilliams, his son Mike McWilliams and grandson Glenn McWilliams. The first Glenn played for the Owls as a center and linebacker from 1943 to 1946. Mike was a center and defensive end for Hondo from 1973 through 1976. His son, Glenn, was an Owl wide receiver and defensive back from 2000 through 2003.

Skipping southeast to Cuero, there are three families having three different generations wearing the Gobbler green and white. All of my information about them came from the late Mike Weber, whose family has owned the Ford dealership since 1937. Weber is responsible for the museum at the Cuero Chamber of Commerce office dedicated to Gobbler football. Mike's family is one of those three generation families. It started with his dad, Cliff, who played end in 1922 and 1923. Thirty years later, Mike was a halfback on the 1952 and 1953 teams. His son, Cliff was a strong safety on the 1974 and 1975 teams. His final game was the loss to Ennis 13-10 in the 1975 State Championship game. That loss snapped the 44-game win streak which Cuero had begun in 1973. Seven years later, his son Richard played tight end on the 1981 and 1982 teams.

Still another family in Cuero with three generations of Gobbler players are the Reeses. Dr. Raymond Reese, a medical doctor still practicing, was a halfback on the 1952 and 1953 teams. His son, Ray, a local attorney and a member of the KBAR FM broadcast team discussed in the Cuero chapter, played on the 1976 through 1979 teams. Ray's son, Pearson, a wide receiver and kicker, just graduated from Cuero High in 2014.

The third family is the Jacob family. Charles played in 1951 and 1952 as a fullback the first year and a halfback the second year. His son Jeff played on the 1973 and 1974 state champion teams and was an All-District linebacker. Jeff's son, Colton played there from 2009 through 2011. He was a defensive end the first year, defensive end and left tackle the second year, 2010, and defensive end, left tackle and linebacker his senior year in 2011. He made All-District first team on both sides of the ball and was chosen to play in the 2012 Texas High School Coaches Association All-Star game in Fort Worth. He signed to play with Mary Hardin Baylor University after he graduated from Cuero.

In Longview, Joseph Russell Brashear is also a chronicler of Lobo football, just as Mike Weber was in Cuero. His family also has three generations who have played for Longview. Their playing years are scattered over 80 years and includes five family members. It started back in the Depression with Charles Aubrey Brashear, Sr., on the offensive line in 1932 and 1933. His son, Charles Jr., was a manager in 1967, 1968 and 1969. Four years later, Joseph played for the Lobos from 1973 through 1975. He was a fullback and linebacker. There are two grandsons of Charles, Sr., who both served as Lobo ball boys before playing varsity ball. Chase Joseph Brashear was a ball boy for six years from 1995 to 2000 before playing on the varsity as a linebacker in 2004 and 2005. His brother, Aaron Clarke Brashear, had one year of sharing ball boy duty in 2000 and continued to do so the next six years ending his duties in 2006. He had two years on the varsity in 2010 and 2011 as a linebacker and deep snapper.

There was no shortage of outstanding linemen for the Lobos when the Collier family each took their turn as they entered Longview High School. The first member to play was Bobby as an offensive and defensive guard in 1944 and 1945. He was a first team All-State player when he was 15 years old. He played at SMU and then with the Los Angeles Rams. His three brothers followed him; first Pat who was a guard in 1947,1948 and 1949. Pat also played for SMU. After Pat came Joe who was an offensive tackle and defensive end in 1953 and 1954. He played for Kilgore Junior College after graduation from Longview High. The last of the brothers was Mike who played linebacker, center and tackle in 1962, 1963 and 1964. He played for the University of Houston in college. Joe's grandson, Clark Orren, played left tackle on offense in 2011 and 2012. He is now a member of the Texas Longhorns team.

Bobby had four sons who played for Longview: Robert, Glenn, Johnny and Kyle. Johnny was a defensive tackle in 1972. Glenn was a defensive end and offensive guard in 1979 and 1980. Kyle was a guard on the 1975 and 1976 Lobos. Robert played offensive guard in 1968 and 1969. He later played at SMU.

In Cameron, three generations of Riola sons have been Yoemen. The first was Charles Riola, a 220 pound right tackle in 1945-46-47. Then came his four sons playing for the Yoemen. Charles junior played in the late 1960s-early 1970s. then came Peter, a defensive end in the mid 70s. Christopher played in the late 70s. The Riola who told me about his family involvement is Dominick Riola, who played in 1982 and 1983 as a wide receiver and defensive end. He has had four sons to play for the Yoemen. Scott and Tyler played about 2006-08. His twin sons, Dylan and Zach Riola were on the 2009 through the 2012 Yoe teams. Dylan played wide receiver, defensive back and quarterback. Zach was a linebacker/running back for Cameron.

It was another family member that played and coached football who Dominic told me about that brought this story full circle. He mentioned an uncle, Johnny Riola who is enshrined in the North Texas State Hall of Fame for his playing there in 1938-39-40. Dominic told me that as a coach, he helped Waco High win a state championship. That had to be the 1948 Lions that beat my Amarillo Sandies for the state title. Dominic didn't know if he was the head coach for Waco. So I checked the information I had access to thanks to Joe

Lee Smith to find that out for Dominic. Johnny was a head coach for three years winning 26 games and losing only four games. But the first two years he was head coach was at Mart in 1945 and 1946. He had coached Justin Read's grandfather, J.B. Read, in that 11-0-0 season in 1946. It was Justin's pride in three generations of his family playing on Mart undefeated teams that inspired me to write this chapter. Now I had found a connection between the Read family in Mart and the Priola family in Cameron with both families being in this chapter that might not have ever been except for Justin Read speaking up in 2012 and Dominic Priola speaking up June 28, 2014. So like the Reads in Mart, two generations of the Riolas played on state championship teams. And Johnny Riola, the uncle who didn't play for Cameron, coached the first of the Reads at Mart. I found that to be a cool coincidence when I discovered it and it reinforced to me what a unique project it had become to write the story of the winningest teams in Texas high school history.

Temple has two families with three generations of players. One of the proud names in Wildcat history is Keifer Marshall. Jr. As a sophomore, he played center and linebacker for the 1940 Temple team that lost the state championship 20-7 to the Amarillo Sandies. In 1941, he anchored those same two positions as the Wildcats made it back to state, losing to Wichita Falls 13-0. He played on the 1942 team before getting a scholarship to play for the University of Texas. With World War II dominating all that was going on in the country, many players dropped out of college to join a military unit. That was the choice made by Marshall. He enlisted in the U.S. Marine Corps and was sent to the Pacific theatre. Marshall was one of six survivors from his company of 252 Marines that fought in the Battle of Iwo Jima. They were surrounded by the Japanese soldiers and didn't receive reinforcements or supplies for 36 hours. When the war was over, he returned to UT and completed his football career. He married his bride of 66 years, Tammy, in 1948 after meeting her in the Commons on the UT campus.

His son, Keifer Marshall III, was a fullback and linebacker for Temple in 1966 through 1968. His two grandsons, Pat Marshall and Rob Marshall, played for Bob McQueen in the late 90s. Pat was defensive tackle in 1996 through 1998. Rob was an offensive guard on the three varsity teams of 1994, 1995 and 1996.

McQueen had David President on his 1972 team playing tight end, free safety and kicker. Nearly twenty years later, two of his sons were playing for McQueen. Dwharnce "Dutch" President was a three year varsity player as a linebacker from 1989 to 1991. His brother, Daina, joined the Wildcat teams of 1991, 1992 and 1993. He was a defensive end and weak side line backer for the first two years. In 1992, the Wildcats won the Class 4A State Championship. In his senior year in 1993, Daina played strong safety and linebacker. David had a third son, Monto, who played basketball. However, Monto has kept the family participation in Temple football going with his son, Chad, who is entering his third varsity season in 2014 as one of the most anticipated players in Texas. Chad was a wide receiver for the 2012 season, but that wasn't where his talents were best utilized. He is a quarterback who was only able to play two games in 2013 before his season ended with an injury. Now he is expected to lead Temple deeper into the Class 5A playoffs as the signal caller. He has already committed to play for Baylor.

The Chastain family of Brownwood also had three generations playing for the Lions. Grady Chastain was the first generation playing for Brownwood in 1954-55-56. He was versatile as the coaches had him at quarterback, outside linebacker, middle linebacker, halfback and fullback in his three years on the varsity. His son Kirk Chastain came along to play for Gordon Wood in 1977-78-79. Kirk went both sides of the ball as a defensive end and fullback. His son, Luke Chastain played for Brownwood in 2008-09-10. In addition to playing wide receiver and safety, he was the valedictorian of the class of 2011.

Also playing for Brownwood has been three generations of the Croft family. Walter played for Gordon Wood in 1963, 1964 and 1965 as a linebacker. His son, David was a linebacker and tight end on the first three of Randy Allen's teams in 1986, '87,'88. The third generation is represented by Walter's grandson, Mitch Stephens, a quarterback for Bob Shipley's teams in 2009, 2010 and 2011.

The Denbow family has been a big fixture in the Corsicana Tigers list of players, beginning with Don Denbow who played from 1961 to 1963. That 1963 team won the 3A state championship with a 7-0 win over Pharr-San Juan-Alamo. His son, Don Ashley Denbow was initially a wide receiver and defensive back when he began playing on the Tiger varsity in 1988. By the time he reached his senior year, he had added the positions of free safety, kicker and quarterback to his resume. Now the third generation player, Trevor, is beginning his second year on the varsity at strong safety and wide receiver. He was on the varsity as a freshman in 2013, so should have three more seasons on the Tigers.

You might have noticed that two of my schools aren't in this chapter, namely Amarillo and Tyler John Tyler. It's not because I didn't try to locate families in those towns. Especially Amarillo, where I grew up and had first hand knowledge of many athletes who played for the Sandies who were in different generations. But I couldn't connect three or more generations together who played for the Sandies. No one came forward who could help in either Amarillo or Tyler. I am sure that I missed somebody in all twelve schools who belonged in this chapter. It's an honor to be able to dig up the ones I have listed in this chapter. Hopefully more readers in these schools will read this chapter and realize that someone in their families belongs here. Perhaps there will be a way to list them in an addendum later on.

RECOGNITION

With this group of schools, there have been many people who have played a part in them winning as many games as each school has done. This chapter is about them and the recognition they have received in high school. Of course, a lot of them have gone on to receive more recognition in college. The two most prominent from these 12 schools have been the two Heisman Trophy winners, Doak Walker of Highland Park and Earl Campbell of Tyler John Tyler. However, this book is about what happened in high school, so I'm not going to follow any players from these schools for what they did in college, All-American honors, etc. So the focus will be on those players who have been picked to play in the Texas High School Coaches Association All-Star games played each summer at the Texas Coaching School since its inception in 1935. Secondly, a number of players from these 12 teams have been elected to the Texas High School Football Hall of Fame. That list is in this chapter. It is a list that the general public has a chance to make nominations to the selection committee of the nine players chosen each year. Finally, being named a high school All-American player is a rare honor, so I have as many of those in here on who I could find verification of their selection by a publication. Getting that verification has not been an easy job, so there are a few that I have been told made an All-American team that I also include in that group.

Obviously, there are many players who have been chosen to Texas All-State teams over the years, too many in fact to single out to name. It would be a list of well over 1,000 names. There is a website you can go to for those names if you want to see them. It has been compiled by a basketball coach out of Belton, Billy Wilbanks. His website is http:/www.texasallstatefootball.com/. There are more than 23,000 names of Texas high school players who have made one or more All-State football teams on his list. The selection of high school All-American football teams really came into being over 60 years ago when Prep Football Magazine began making selections. In 1963, Parade Magazine began putting out its lists. Then 34 years ago, USA Today started putting out its own list. There are a few players from these schools who have won these honors. They are named in the final two lists in this chapter.

Anyway, I am starting with the Coaching School players. They are all graduated seniors by the time they play in this game usually in July following their graduation. Many of them had already committed to colleges to play by this time. But for some, it will be the last time in their lives that they don shoulder pads and a helmet. That they get to play before the biggest gathering of high school football coaches in the world makes this game that much more special an honor Presented here in alphabetical order by each school and by the earliest year going forward are the Texas high school players who were All-Stars then and still are today in the minds of their fans.

Amarillo: 1935-Red Stidger, 1936-Frank Brunson, 1937-Robert Clesson, 1938-Harold King, 1939-Stanley Mauldin, Bill Thompson, 1940-Charlie Gill, 1941-Myrtle Greathouse, W.C. Wooten, 1942-Burrell Collins, 1943-Jimmy Blesson, 1944-Billy Lynch, 1946-Bill Juett, 1947-Harland Collins, 1948-Sam Attebury, 1950-Jack Newby, 1951-Howard Childers, 1953-Louis Flores, 1957-Roy Northrup, 1958-David Russell, 1961-George Tiffany, 1970-Bobby Giles, 1972-Rick Fenlaw, 1977-Carl Birdsong, 1978-Dan Reed, 1990-Matt Breckbill, 1996-Detrick Johnson, 1997-Dan Belcher, 1998-Trans Holland, 2006-Brad McCarty

Brownwood: 1937-James Thomason, Bill Miller, 1941-Jim Edison, 1948-Don Wright, 1950-Dan Low, 1953-Leondous Fry, 1954-Ray Masters, 1961-Lawrence Elkins, 1963-Terry Southall, 1965-James Harris, 1966-Joe Shaw, 1968-Bob Rothe, 1969-Lane Bowen, 1970-Jimmy Carmichael, 1971-Gene Day, 1972-Shae Southall, 1975-Tony Jones, 1977-Doug Reid, 1978-Eddie Gill, 1979-Scott Lancaster, 1980-Kirk Chastain, 1982-Mike Kinsey, 1983-Marvin Rathke, 1988-Steve Mosley, 1994-James Allred, 1999-Colby Freeman, 2002-Brett Valde, 2003-Freddie Stoglin, 2005-Lee Grime

Cameron Yoe: 1944-Frank Torra, 1945-Robert Terry, 1949-Robert Zotz, 1965-Mike Perrin, 1966-Mack McKinney, 1970-Ronnie Richardson, 1976-Joe Smitherman, 1980-Terry Lowe, 1982-Bill Huffman, 1983-Nelson Huffman, 1984-Sam Scott, 1986-Kyle Kruse, 1987-Seth Dockery, 1988-Paul Johnson, 1997-Paul Hooks, 2003-Billy Pittman, 2005-Ryan Mullins, 2006-Marcus Zaranksy, 2008-Thomas Limmer, 2011-Jack Rhoades, 2013-Edgar Luna, 2014-Somari Wright

Corsicana: 1935-Otha Langston, Paul Harshaw, 1936-Robert Nelson, Tom Sharp, 1937-R. Everette, 1940-Wallace Spencer, 1942-Felto Perwitt, 1950-Howard Chamberlin, 1951-Duane Nutt-1962-John H. Tewas, 1964-Jim Hagle, 1971-Jeff Jobe, 1983-Kent Tramel, 1985-Bill Jones, 1987-Mike Sims, 1989-Brad Powell, 1995-Willie Bradley, 1996-Ketric Sanford, 1998-Billy Yates, 2005-Jon Bauer

Cuero: 1939-Lewis Mayne, 1942-B. Kuehl, 1952-Fred Hansen, 1971-Henry Sheppard, 1974-Arthur Whittington, 1975-David Hill, 1977-Joe Campbell, 1986-Brad Goebel, 1987-Brian Parks, 1988-Carl Taylor, 1991-Omar Littles, 1992-Doug Hughes, 1994-Brad Schley, 1996-Clint Finley, 2000-Marcus Screws, 2003-Cody Wallace, 2005-Ross Nigh, 2006-J.T. Rudd, 2008-Quincy Whittington, 2009-Klayton Smith, 2010-Tyler Arndt, 2011-Tanner Hoffman, 2012-Jacob Colton

Highland Park: 1935-Arthur Wimmer, William Thomasson, Hale Cornelius, 1936-Nelson Hughes, 1938-David Gay, 1939-Jack Swank, Hugh Munnell, 1944-Douglas McDonalds, Bobby Layne, 1945-Harold Clark, 1946-Bill Elliott, Jimmy Flowers, 1949-Bill Crisler, 1950-Jack Archibald, 1951-Ed Benet, 1955-Tom Gray, 1958-Jack Collins, 1960-William Cannon, 1966-Deryl Comer, 1977-Scott Smith, 1974-Lott McIlhenny, 1980-Lance McIlhenny, 1981-John Barns, 1984-David Richards, 1985-John Stollenwerch, 1988-Dale Smith, 2006-Chris Olson, 2008-Seth Gardner, 2009-Jeff Howeth, 2011-Jake Howeth, 2013-William Burns, 2014-Tony Richards

Hondo: 1945-Odie Gilliam, 1947-Blanton Taylor, 1956-Jerry Muennink, 1957-Alvin Hartmann, 1971-Morris Faseler, 1982-Rowdy Moos

Longview: 1937-Preston Simms, 1938-Ted Brannon, Chal Daniel, 1941-Don Fambrough, 1944-Forest Griggs, 1945-Clarence McGaw, 1946-Bobby Collier, 1948-Don Menasco, 1951-Billy Jones, 1952-Bobby Blakely, 1959-George Hogan, 1964-Jackie Howe, 1968-David Walters, 1974-Mike Mock, 1976-Henry Williams, 1977-Hosea Taylor, 1992-Bobby Taylor, 1998-Lee Jackson, 2006-Vondrell McGee, 2007-Sherman Roseborough, 2008- Blake Bledsoe, 2009-LaMarcus Howard, 2010-Aaron Johnson, 2011-Javorious Brown, 2012-Eric Hawkins, 2013-Cornelius Williams, 2014-DeRodrick Alexander

Mart: 1937-Curtis Sandig, 1938-Cullin Rogers, 1942-Roy Smith, 1958-Alfred Glockzin, 1959-Jerry Hopkins, 1977-James Medlock, 1985-Tony Baker, 1987-Darren Nobles, 1988-Lee Miles, 2000-John Garrett, 2001-Rick Lane, 2002-Quincy Cosby, 2007-Landen Summers, 2009-Colby Summers, 2011-D'Shun Kinsey, 2013-Quentin Bryant

Plano: 1954-Bobby Teer, 1962- David Graves, 1964-Gerald Lewis, 1967-Kenneth Davis, 1968-John Griggs, 1971-Mike Crowell, 1972-Pat Thomas, 1973-Rucker Lewis, 1976-Sammy Buckham, 1978-C.M.Pier, 1979-Billy Ray Smith, 1986-Terry Price, 1987-Brad Gurney, 1988-Steve Needham, 194-Clint Snowden, 1995-Scooter Asel, 2008-Blake McJunkin, 2009-Carson Meger, 2010-Grant Pierce

Temple: 1935-Ki Aldrich, 1936-Jody Market, 1937-Alvin Moeller, 1938-Euel Wesson, Noble Doss, 1939-Tom Pickett, 1940-A.J. Mercer, 1941-thelbert Hardt, Ed Dusek, 1942-Ed Heap, Wayland Hill, 1943-Keifer Marshall, Dan Fergus,

1945-Red Simmons, 1947-George Gentry, 1949-Vernon Barron, 1950-Roy Pace, 1951-Richard E. Black, 1952-Bill Green, 1953-Doyle Traylor, 1955-Charles Caffrey, 1956-Lee Benner, 1957-Billy Zalenski, 1958-Dan Malin, 1959-Bobby Wooley, Brad Dusek, 1974-Alfred Sanders, 1976-Doug Streater, 1977-Robert Caughlan, 1979-Mike Weddington, 190-Adrian Simpson, 1987-Gayle Beard, 1993-Greg Steele, 2009-Brett Gun, 2012-Tion Briggs, 2013-Freddie Johnson, 2014-James Judie

Tyler John Tyler: 1936-James Daniel, 1939-Alfred Temple, 1940-Walton Roberts, 1942-Wayne Burnet, 1945-Dillard Hart, 1947- Billy Porter, 1951-Eddie Hennig, 1953-MikeTrant, 1955-Charles Milstead, 1960-Tim Faulkner, 1974-Earl Campbell, 1975-Ronnie Lee, 1976-Zach Guthrie, 1980-Keith Guthrie, 1991-Joey Ellis, 1995-Mart Broyles, 2000-Lennis Smith, 2001-Aaron Ross, 2002-William Blaylock, 2006-Kerry Maddox

Those that have been chosen for the Texas High School Football Hall of Fame are listed below from the earliest honorees to the most recent selections in this section. In addition to the players, coaches and sportswriters clearly identified with covering one of the 12 teams are identified in this section. There is an eleven year gap in the selections made at the Texas High School Hall of Fame in Waco that stretches from 1973 through 1983. During that time, the Hall was moved to Breckinridge before coming back to Waco. There was no voting for new Hall members while it was in Breckenridge.

In order of the years chosen beginning in 1969 continuing until now, here are the players, coaches and sportswriters inducted into the Texas High School Sports Hall of Fame.

1969-Chal Daniel, Longview 1935-37; Bobby Wilson, Corsicana 1929-31

1970- Stan Mauldin, Amarillo 1936-38

1972-Burl Bufkin, Amarillo 1928-30

1973-Bobby Layne, Highland Park 1941-43; Billy Stamps, Corsicana 1928-30; Doak Walker Highland Park 1942-45

1983-Ki Aldrich, Temple 1932-34; Earl Campbell, Tyler John Tyler1971-73

1984-Barton "Botchey" Koch, Temple 1924-26; Putt Powell, Amarillo sportswriter; Gordon Wood, Brownwood coach 1940-85

1985-Doyle Traylor, Temple 1950-52

1986-Rusty Russell, Masonic Home, Highland Park coach 1922-45

1987-Blair Cherry, Amarillo coach 1932-36; Lawrence Elkins, Brownwood 1958-60

1988- W.W. Windy Nicklaus, Amarillo 1921-23

1989-Pete Shotwell, coach at Abilene, Longview, Breckenridge 1916-52; Billy Ray Smith, Plano 1977-79

1990-Eck Curtis, coach at Anson, Ranger, Breckenridge and Highland Park,1945

1992-Jimmy Carmichael, Brownwood 1967-69; Jack Collins, Highland Park 1956-57

1993-John Clark, coach Plano 1957-76

1994-Morris Southall, coach, Brownwood, 1947-86

1995-Noble Doss, Temple 1935-37; Maco Stewart, Corsicana 1930-31

1996-Buster Gilbreth, Cuero coach 1957-80; Myrtle Greathouse, Amarillo 1939-40;Tom "Meal Ticket" Pickett, Temple 1936-38;David Richards, Highland Park 1980-83; the Southall brothers: Terry, Shea, Si- Brownwood-special recognition

1998-Lance McIlhenny, Highland Park 1976-79; Charles Milstead, Tyler 1953-55; Alfred "Big Un" Rose, Highland Park 1923; Wallace H. Scott, Jr., Tyler 1935-38

1999-James Street, Longview 1963-66; Euel "Tiny" Wesson, Temple 1935-37; Bill Stovall, Brownwood sports writer

2000-Jay Stanley Fikes, Lufkin, Temple coach 1943-63; Loyd Phillips, Longview 1960-62;Jim Thomason, Brownwood, 1934-36

2001-Frank Bevers, Highland Park coach 1974-82, 89-92; Bobby Dillon, Temple 1945-47

2003-Jerry Hopkins, Mart 1956-58; Tommy Vaughan, Brownwood 1934-36

2004-Ed Bernet, Highland Park 1949-50; Mike Kinsey, Brownwood 1980-81; Ronnie Lee, Tyler 1972-74

2006-Bob McQueen, Mexia, Temple coach 1972-99

2007-Bret Stafford, Temple, Belton 1979-82

2009-Kenneth Davis, Temple 1979-81

2010-Sammy Baugh, Sweetwater, Temple 1930-32

2011-Quan Cosby, Mart 1998-2000

2012-Bobby Taylor, Longview 1989-91

The Parade All-American list begins with Brownwood quarterback Jimmy Carmichael and his wide receiver Perry Young on the Lions in 1969. The next player selected was running back Earl Campbell of Tyler John Tyler in 1973. Six years later, Lance McIlhenny of Highland Park was recognized in 1979. Then in 1982, Brett Stafford who had starred at Temple before transferring to Belton when his dad began coaching there was selected to the Parade list. A year later in 1983, offensive lineman David Richards of Highland Park was selected as the Parade Magazine National High School Player of the Year. In 2005, Highland Park quarterback Matthew Stafford was chosen to the list.

Richards has been the only player from these 12 schools selected to two different high school All-American teams as he also made the USA Today 1983 team. There are five more players from schools featured in *Friday's Winners* who have been selected to the USA Today list since Richards. Defensive back Bobby Richards of Longview was chosen in 1991. Five years later in 1996, David Warren of Tyler John Tyler was chosen as a defensive lineman. It was another 12 years before another player, offensive lineman Stavion Lowe of Brownwood was picked to the 2008 second offensive team. Lache Sestrunk of Temple was a first team running back in 2009. In 2011, DeMarkus Latham of Longview was a second team choice to the defensive team as a linebacker.

Charles Milstead of Tyler was chosen for the Prep Football Magazine All-American Honor Roll in 1956. The magazine was published once a year by Kurt Lenser of Alhambra, California. He named players from virtually every state to his list as well as the Territory of Hawaii since it would be three years before it became a state. Alaska was also a territory, but had no players selected. He especially liked Milstead and put his picture on the cover of the 1956 edition as the Outstanding Player in Texas for 1955. Prep Football Magazine is no longer published as Mr Lenser is listed as being 105 years old now and presumably retired. Anyway efforts to locate him or family members who could give a more detailed history of how long Prep Football was published were unsuccessful.

Likewise, the lists of All-American players chosen by Parade Magazine were incomplete. I could only find a list of 200 players chosen by the magazine for the 51 years it has been published. Since the magazine selects at least 22 players a year, that leaves over 900 players of which there could be more players from teams in *Friday's Winners* that I have left out of this chapter. But emails and phone messages to Parade's New York City headquarters to learn more were never answered.

So, here are some players who have been named to someone's All-American team who deserve to be there, but the verification of their honor was lacking: James Garner, Amarillo High -1948; Quan Cosby, Mart High-1999; Steve Judy, Longview High-1967; and Ketric Sanford, Corsicana-1995. Cosby might have been a USA Today honoree or a Parade Magazine honoree, Judy a Prep Football Magazine honoree and Sanford a Parade Magazine honoree.

THE AMARILLO SANDIES

FIRST YEAR THEY PLAYED: 1908
ALL TIME RECORD THROUGH 2013: 743-337-22
WINNING PERCENTAGE: 68.42%
PLAYOFF APPEARANCES: 52
STATE CHAMPIONSHIP GAMES WON: 1934, 1935, 1936, 1940
STATE CHAMPIONSHIP GAMES LOST: 1930, 1948

First, the football and all other athletic teams at AHS were called the Savages. That continued until the spring of 1922 when baseball coach Charles Douglass, inspired by the dust storm in which his Amarillo players were practicing commented how they reminded him of a golden sandstorm. Thus, one of the great mascot names was chosen from that simple comment. The Golden Sandstorm evolved into the Golden Sandies and into the Sandies. Today all three versions of that mascot name are used in describing the athletic teams and student body of Amarillo High. Soon, a cartoon character resembling a sand storm with a ferocious face began to show up on the sports pages of the Amarillo Globe-News. The mascot continues to evolve into newer versions today, all of which along with the other traditions established over the years makes being a Sandie a special privilege and honor. In 2009, my Amarillo High graduating class held its 50th anniversary. I was asked to write about our experiences a half century earlier for our 50 year reunion. My comments reflect some of my thoughts of what it means to be a Sandie. Here is the last paragraph of those comments to give you a feel of what being a Sandie is all about.

"Yes, I admit to getting chills seeing the Sandie colors of black and gold still to this day. I get pumped when I hear a band, nowadays usually the Tech band or the UT band, strike up 'Grandioso,' a tune that I consider Sandie property. I am grateful for having had those days at AHS and making the friendships that I did which still go on to this day. I hope all of you feel the same way. Once a Sandie, always a Sandie!"

It's one thing for me, an old grad to have those feelings. However experiencing the Sandie tradition is also one that a newcomer can immediately be immersed in. Here is a blog written in August 2011 by the Reverend Allan Stanglin who had just moved to Amarillo to join the staff of Central Church of Christ that month. His two daughters became students at Amarillo High immediately. His blog was written shortly after he and his wife Carrie-Anne attended the pep rally at Amarillo High that was the kickoff of the Sandie football season, an opening game with Midland High. This is what he had to say about being exposed to and becoming part of the Sandie tradition.

"There's something really cool about being a part of this Amarillo High School scene. It's the sense of genuine community. I'm sure it has a lot to do with the history of the place. Amarillo High has been around since 1889. There's a lot of tradition here. In fact, they do all they can to keep the traditions alive. They still use the old 1920s mascot and logos on much of their literature and publications. They still employ a quaint rally chant from the 40s, 'Blow Sand, Blow!' at opportune times during football games. While discussing tonight's tailgating activities in the parking lot after the pep rally, we met a couple of people who went to school at AHS, sent their kids to AHS, and now have grandchildren here on the football team and on the spirit squads. There's a lot of that here. They value their history. They uphold their traditions. When you're a member of the Amarillo High School community, you're part of something much bigger than yourself. You're a part of something that's been vital and important since before your grandparents were born and something that'll be vital and important long after you're gone."

With that explanation of how the Golden Sandstorm came to be and how the traditions are embraced today by both old and new Sandies, here is a look at how the football teams over the years have made the Sandie record what it is today. It starts in the year 1951, looks backward, then forward and ends with how the Sandies were looking for the 2014 season.

Early in 1951, the Amarillo School Board chose not to renew Howard "Bull" Lynch's contract as head football coach of the Amarillo Golden Sandstorm. Lynch had been head coach there since 1937, the year after Blair Cherry ended his seven year run as the Sandies' head coach with an 84-5 record. His teams won the A State Championships in 1934-35-36. Lynch had been Cherry's assistant during that remarkable run. Lynch went on to gain another State Championship as his Sandies beat Temple in 1940. In 1942, the Sandies reached the State Semi-Finals before falling to Dallas Sunset. In 1948, he had his Sandies back in a State Championship game which they lost to Waco 21-0. In all through the 1950 season, his Sandies compiled a record of 126-29-1 in 14 years with Lynch at the helm.

But then came the 1950 season. The Sandies went 4-6. It was the first time since 1926 that they had failed to win at least seven games in a season. Despite his very impressive credentials in leading the Sandies for 14 years, the school board acted to either not renew his contract or to force him to resign or whatever. Lynch would move into administration becoming the assistant principal at the Polk Street campus of Amarillo High before becoming principal of Tascosa High School when it opened in 1958. Nevertheless, his non-renewal raised eyebrows around the state. His firing or whatever act was done by the Amarillo school board drew lots of talk all over Texas. The Austin American Statesman mentioned that it was the result of a whisper campaign begun in Amarillo by disgruntled fans. The Statesman even went on to jokingly say that the Texas Interscholastic League (the UIL) was an organization that had been established for the sole purpose of providing high school football teams to lose to Amarillo.

That might have been the mindset of most every football fan and coach all over Texas given the record the Sandies had rolled up during that run of 23 straight years of seven plus wins. Where the nation had been in the Great Depression since 1929 that wouldn't end until the country began to recover after the end of World War II, Sandie football was in its own bull market as measured by the wins, district titles and advancements into the playoffs. The teams of Hugh Butler, Dutch Smith, Cherry and Lynch achieved a 234-32-2 record during that time. Percentage wise, that amounted to the Sandies winning 87.3% of all their games during this run. By comparison, since I began researching and writing this book, the one team I most get asked about is Odessa Permian. Friday Night Lights, the book, the movie and the television series has made it famous all over the country. Everyone who asks thinks that Permian has to be one of the teams in Friday's Winners given their record. During the Panthers history, they have won 75.75% of their games. They started playing in 1960 and despite their tremendous success still trail in total wins, over 200 behind the top leaders of Highland Park, Amarillo, Plano, Temple, Brownwood and Mart.

Going back to the stock market analogy mentioned above, the bull market ended for the Sandies football fortunes starting with that 4-6 record during Bull Lynch's final season. Though no one knew it yet, the Sandies were entering a 26 year bear market in which they would accumulate a 145-114-7 record. Just like in the regular stock market, there were spikes of prosperity such as the 1956 and 1957 years of Joe Kerbel, the 1959 season of Bum Phillips and the

1967 year of Warren Harper. Those coaches took the Sandies to the playoffs just those four times in that quarter century span. Unfortunately my senior year's football season, 1958, would be the worst ever for the Sandies. We went 2-8. The 1973 team matched us with only two wins, but managed to salvage two ties for a 2-6-2 mark. The 1961, 1962, 1971 and 1974 Sandies all finished with just three wins for their seasons. Still after 51 years since the streak began in 1927, the Sandies were 379-146-9 having won 70.9% of their games. This bear market streak might be characterized in geological or religious terms as having occurred following the Post C-L era and before the WWD era. C-L stands for Cherry-Lynch and WWD is an acronym for Winning With Dipple. We didn't know it then, but when Larry Dipple came on board as the Sandie head coach in 1975 through 2005, the appropriate theme song might have been that bottom of the Depression era classic, "Happy Days are Here Again."

But going back to the early days of success, it would be appropriate to say that Blair Cherry was the architect of that success. He depended on his field generals, i.e. his quarterbacks, to carry out his plans on the field. Back then, high school football teams had only two or so coaches at the most. Not at all like it is today with 4A teams and up sporting pictures of up to 14 coaches in the football programs. There were no head-sets connecting the head coach with offensive and defensive coordinators who were seeing the field below from high atop or inside the press box yelling rapid-fire instructions as they watch the action below and reacting accordingly. The quarterbacks during Cherry's successful run at Amarillo High were on their own to call the plays as they saw fit. A major factor in that freedom given them by Cherry was in the formation he chose for them to run, the double wing back.

I learned this on July 12, 2012 when I went to Tyler to meet and interview Johnny "Red" Stidger. Stidger was the quarterback on the 1934 State Champion Sandies. That was his senior year. He played for SMU for three years. Now 97, Stidger continues to live in his own home alone since his wife of 69 years, Madaleine, died four years earlier. He gets out to drive his car around Tyler being careful not to "get on the Interstate" in his own words. A year earlier, he quit playing golf for health reasons. But two weeks before we met, he had a new pacemaker installed. It was making him feel pretty good and he was at least thinking about getting out on the links again. He became the first double interviewee for me since he was also the head coach of the Tyler Lions from 1958-68. That portion of my interview with him will be in the chapter on Tyler.

His recollection of his days at Amarillo High, Coach Cherry and the games he played in are as clear today as if it was during the spring semester of his senior year in 1935. He began telling me about the 1933 Sandies, a team in which he was the backup quarterback to J.R. Corbett. That team went 10-0 behind the great athleticism and leadership of Corbett. When the regular season play ended, it was discovered that Corbett had been ineligible the entire season due to his having turned 19 before September 1933. The Sandies were replaced in the playoffs by the district runner-up Pampa Harvesters. One of the key wins for the Sandies in that year was a 7-6 narrow victory over the Lubbock Westerners. Stidger kicked the winning extra point in that game. It was a forerunner of some key kicks he would make in 1934.

He commented what it was like to play for Coach Cherry. "He was a good coach. He really worked us hard. If he wasn't happy with the way we practiced, he had us immediately go to the practice field next door where the Amarillo College Badgers played and have a scrimmage with them. He was a master of the game. He had a lot of razzle dazzle in the plays he drew up." He reflected further, "We played Corpus Christi for the State Championship at the Cotton Bowl. Coach Cherry wanted to make sure nothing kept us from playing our best. So he carried 50 gallons of Amarillo water to Dallas for the team to drink so we wouldn't get sick drinking strange water as we prepared for the game."

I had brought a list of all the Amarillo game results for the two years he played to the interview. I just had to mention the opponent and he nailed the score, calling it out to me with very few misses. Sometimes he was off by a point or two, but he remembered how the season went with remarkable accuracy 78 years after playing in the games. As he said, Coach Cherry left it up to him to call the plays and execute them. There was little subbing players in with new plays or having him run to the sidelines for quick instructions between plays. One game that he recalled in particular was the Lubbock High game. The Sandies won it 25-0. Stidger scored all the points in the game. He said, "I kept running the bootleg. The Westerners couldn't stop it. So I handled the ball most of the time not needing to hand off to one of my backs." The results were four touchdowns and one extra point kick by the 138 pound redhead during the game. In the final district game against Pampa, he threw a 44 yard touchdown pass to John Peterson to break a 6-6 tie. He kicked the extra point for a 13-6 Amarillo victory.

He remembered the playoff games being very tough. In Bi-District, they squeezed past Ranger 19-14. They toppled Big Spring 31-20 in the Quarter-Finals. The Semi-Final game was the toughest of all as the Sandies at home hosted the Masonic Home squad made famous in Jim Dent's book, *12 Mighty Orphans*. In the 1932 Semi-Final game, the Masonic Home beat the Sandies 7-6. This was the chance for payback. Stidger picks up the story,"Those were the toughest guys we ever played. There were only 13 on their team, 11 on the field and two on the bench. Five times, we drove inside their 10 yard line, but they kept us out of the end zone. Finally, late in the game, we got down to their 15. (It actually was the third play of the fourth quarter on the Masonic Home 14 yard line.) That was close enough and about as far as I could kick the ball. Back then the goal posts were on the end zone line. So I lined up and kicked the field goal that scored the only points in the game." The weather might have contributed since the game was played at Butler Field in Amarillo with the temperature at 11 degrees and snow on the ground.

With that 3-0 win over Masonic Home, the Sandies were State Champion game bound. They were to face the heavily favored Corpus Christi Buccaneers, also undefeated with a 12-0 record at the Cotton Bowl in Dallas four days after Christmas on December 29, 1934. Corpus Christi got there early enough to be practicing in the Cotton Bowl on Christmas Day. The Buccaneers not only brought their own band, but six other high school bands around the Gulf Coast accompanied them to Dallas. They all took the train on a round trip special ticket of $4.20 per person from Corpus to Dallas and back. That price sounds today like an unbelievable bargain, but keep in mind, the Depression was going all out, jobs were hard to come by, families were financially pressed to stay together (that is why the Masonic Home and its ilk such as the IOOF Home in Corsicana were taking in so many orphans during this time) and $4.20 railroad tickets were a fortune to many fans. Likewise, the Amarillo fans and the Sandies football team took the train to Dallas. In all, it was reported there were 21,986 paying customers that entered the Cotton Bowl on December 29 to see the two teams battle for the title.

Before the game kicked off, even the Sandie coaches were in awe of the Buccaneers team. Stidger recalled that they were in a pre game huddle. He said, "Coach Cherry looked over at the Corpus Christi bench and exclaimed, 'Good Lord, those guys are big!'" The Buccaneers had the great running back, Charles Haas who had been regularly running between 100 to 200 yards a game over each of the 12 teams that had gone down to defeat to Corpus Christi.

Against the Sandies, it looked initially as if he would continue that streak. Stidger said, "He ran for three first downs plus on his first three carries of the game." Then the Sandies settled in on defense. Haas was shut down the rest of the game. At the end of the shocking 48-0 upset win, the Sandies had rolled up 464 rushing yards and 27 first downs to 81 rushing yards and 12 first downs for the Buccaneers. "The plays drawn up by Cherry worked," recalled Stidger. Glenn Bufkin, a starting back for the Sandies scored two touchdowns during the rout. Back home in Amarillo, his wife delivered their first son during the second quarter of the game. Perhaps the last baby born in Amarillo in 1934.

In side bar items about the impact of the game carried in the Amarillo newspapers, it was mentioned that the game was heard on the radio deep into

Mexico that day. It also was reported in a Nashville, Tennessee newspaper that day. Back then, that was considered amazing that game coverage could extend that far in either medium. Today of course, sports coverage is worldwide and live via television and radio and the Internet as those who had been rising at 4:00 a.m. in August of 2012 to watch Olympic events in London live can attest. (More about the current trends of media coverage in the chapter on the Cuero Gobblers.)

Out of that State Championship win came several honors and a scholarship for Stidger. He was named the second team All-State quarterback. That incensed the Amarillo newspaper writer, Gene Howe, who was called Old Tack. He wrote a column called the Tackless Texan. He maintained in his column that Stidger got gypped by the selection committee by not choosing him first team All-State. He was chosen to play in the first Texas High School Coaches All-Star game in 1935, the first of 30 Sandies to gain that honor so far. Maybe the most amazing thing was the way in which he and three of his Sandie teammates got scholarships to play for SMU. In addition to Stidger, Cliff Matthews, a guard, John Harland, a running back and John L. Sullivan, a center were signed to play for the Ponies. Stidger recalled, "I never even talked with a SMU coach. Coach Cherry arranged with Mattie Bell, the SMU coach for us to get those scholarships and told us about them afterwards." With the Depression in full swing, transportation was an issue for many people. Stidger told his son-in-law, Mike Sipe, that when it came time for the Sandie signees to report to SMU to begin training camp, Coach Blair Cherry drove them to Dallas. Getting back to Amarillo during vacations and summer breaks involved using the thumb to hitch rides, the tried and true way to travel back then. Sipe told me about that part of Stidger's college experience in a recent phone conversation in August 2014.

The way in which Stidger, Matthews, Harland and Sullivan got scholarships to play college football is quite a contrast to the recruiting wars and publicity profiles of future college players of today that begin in some cases as early as the eighth grade. There are a myriad of rules now on when a college coach can make contact with those players they covet, even as to when they can go attend their high school games just to watch them play. But the correspondence from the colleges that is now allowed comes fast and furious to top football players. There is even the uglier side of rogue agents inserting themselves into the recruiting process today for big cash payments from colleges as profiled in Curtis Bryan's article, "The Negotiation" in the August 2012 issue of Texas Monthly. Noting Stidger's composure and easy going manner, I would bet that he would have handled the recruiters of today as well as he handled the defenses of the 1934 Sandie opponents.

We skip ahead 23 years to what I consider the most talented Sandie team ever, the 1957 edition coached by Joe Kerbel. Admittedly, I was in school with them that year, so I do have some prejudice and bias for what they brought to the table in terms of speed, strength, finesse and outright accomplishment on the field. Kerbel arrived on the scene to replace Bill Defee who replaced Lynch for the four years from 1951-54. Defee barely had a winning record for his time at the helm of the Sandies. There were no playoff appearances during his stay. Kerbel had just coached Breckenridge to the 1953 and 1954 Class A state championships. He appeared to be the anointed one to lead Amarillo back into its glory days.

Though he was rotund in shape, he demanded that his players be totally physically fit. And to back up his demands, he staged grueling workouts that drove the players to exhaustion. He had an extremely loud voice, very gruff, by which he made his demands and criticisms of his players. There was very little that escaped his notice. Despite his obvious appetite for fattening food, Kerbel also demanded of his players to lay off any foods that could harm them in any way. One big restriction that he had in place by the time I got there for the 1956 season was the eating of sweets. All sweets of any kind were strictly verboten. His dictates to the team on the subject were known throughout the student body. What he said was the law of the land. Nobody was supposed to break this very strict rule on not eating sweets. So I was shocked one morning when someone brought a bag of small cinnamon rolls from the bakery across Polk Street from AHS to a journalism class where Billy Hulett and I were in class together. Hulett was a senior and a halfback on the Sandies. When the rolls were passed around the room, Hulett took one of those little rolls and devoured it without a pang of guilt. I was shocked that one of Kerbel's key players would break such a strict rule. It appeared to be sacrilege at its worst. Given Kerbel's reputation for losing his temper and being mean to his players for any infraction of his rules, let alone messing up a play in practice or an actual game, I was worried for Billy's wellbeing should Kerbel ever find out how Hulett violated this one rule one time for a taste of a relatively small cinnamon roll.

Anyway, the Sandies broke even at 5-5 in the 1955 season, Kerbel's first at AHS. In 1956, when Hulett was eating the illicit sweet, the Sandies went 9-2. The season ended in a rematch in Bi-District with Fort Worth Paschal, a team the Sandies had rolled past easily in non-district. To say we were looking ahead might be an understatement. The focus was definitely on meeting the next opponent, Abilene. Beating Paschal again would be a no brainer or so we thought. The shocking loss we suffered at their hands in Bi-District might have been the first time that I realized how right was the phrase, "On any given ——", (You fill in the day of choice. Friday, Saturday or Sunday) there is no telling when one football team can rise up and knock off another one favored to beat it."

Before the 1957 season began, the prognosticators all over the state were predicting redemption for the Sandies in addition to a State Championship title. Back then, when the Texas High School Coaching School took place in late July, the votes were collected at the Coaching School as to who the media and coaches thought would be the state champions in all classes. The Sandies were, hands down the overwhelming favorite to take it all in Class 4A, in the process ending the winning streak of the Abilene Eagles. Under Chuck Moser and featuring players such as Glenn Gregory, Abilene had duplicated the Sandies' feat of 1934-35-36 of winning three straight state championships in 1954-55-56. But the Sandies were loaded with future college players and even drew the votes to be #1 in mythical national polls.

They opened the season with 10 straight wins, allowing their opponents only 23 points total while they rolled up 430 points. Joe Kerbel's troops took revenge on Paschal in the second game of the season 34-7. Just like the year before, Paschal was their opponent in Bi-District. There was no slipup this time. Paschal fell for the second time of the year to the Sandies 26-6. A Quarter-Final match with Abilene was next on the agenda. Kerbel won the coin flip and got to choose the Sandies' home field, Dick Bivins Stadium as the site of the game. The build up and hype for the game was big all over Texas. Bivins Stadium had seating for 15,000 fans. But so many wanted to see this game that somehow seating was found for over 22,000 fans to be there for the December 7 showdown. Fans were seated on the track oval in folding chairs around the field. It was to be, even 57 years later, the largest crowd ever to see a game in Amarillo.

Amarillo was heavily favored and scored the first touchdown only to see Abilene tie it up still in the first quarter. The Sandies scored again to lead 14-7. Abilene answered once more and the teams went into halftime tied 14-14. The Eagles did all the scoring in the second half for a 33-14 win to run their consecutive win streak to 49 games. Highland Park would end it for the Eagles the next week in the State Semi-Finals as the Scots went on to win the 1957 AAAA State Championship on December 21 winning 21-9 over Port Arthur. Back in Amarillo, there was a pall that spread over the fans on the Amarillo side of Dick Bivins. It was even rumored, but never confirmed that one gambler lost his house betting on the Sandies. I was in the press box and wrote the following comment about what happened after the end of the game, "I remember leaving the press box a few minutes after the game ended. The press box opened on the south end and in making my exit, I noticed a giant sandstorm bearing down on the field from the southwest. I thought to myself, "What a headline. The Sandstorm arrived late today."

But there was still one silver lining for the 1957 Sandies that became apparent when the season ended. They were so talented, so tough, so strong and so fast that virtually everyone on the team got recruited to play football or run track in college, mostly at Division I schools. There were 30 players out of 40 on that team that were recruited to play at the next level. All but two of the offers came from Division I colleges. To my knowledge, only the 1995 Dallas Carter team had nearly that many players recruited. There were 18 seniors that got scholarships that year. The juniors and sophomores on the team that would get athletic scholarship offers would be divided in the 1958 season into either Sandies or Tascosa Rebels as the new school fielded its first team, splitting AHS's enrollment nearly in half. The 1957 Sandies and the schools they were recruited for included: Texas Tech- Soapy Sudury, Dickie Polson, Charlie Rice, Ken Kendrick, Durwood Epps;Texas-David Russell, Tommy York, Gene Gifford, Mal Whitsett, Curry Bechtol, Don Broome;Oklahoma-Bill White, Tom Cox, Keith Lafon, Danny Jordan; SMU-Buddy Clayton, Joe Ted Davidson, New Mexico State-Allen Sepkowitz, Phil Ehly, Doug Veazey, J. W. Witt, Dale Alexander, Chris Cadenhead;Texas A & M-Barry Ward; TCU-Jerry Spearman;Panhandle A & M-Jerry Stouse, Frank Thompson; Oklahoma State-Jim Means, Eastern New Mexico University-Bill Brooks; Colorado State University-Dick Stovall. The next time that Amarillo would have a double digit win season would be in 1967 as Harper coached them to a 10-1 record.

Perhaps the player from that '57 team that has the most visibility today is Johnny B "Soapy" Sudbury, at least where things that are AHS is concerned. With his involvement in current ongoing Sandie projects, both athletic and otherwise, he connects with the current student body and alumni and booster club organizations in a way that he fits right in to promoting the Sandie way of life. He had plenty to say though about his playing days for the Sandies back in 1955, 56 and 57. Soapy was best known as the quarterback of the Sandies, but also he played defensive back. In 1956, he was the first team All-District quarterback. Strangely in 1957, he was only elected to the second team All-District quarterback despite the fact he was quarterbacking the #1 team in the state that rolled over all its district opponents by big margins. He was an Honorable-Mention All-State at quarterback his senior year. He began talking about the experience of playing for the Sandies, "Amarillo in the fifties was all-in for high school football and we got tremendous support. The civic clubs would request for the coaches and players to be guests at their luncheons and everyone in town made the players feel special."

Then he discussed the five years that he was coached by Kerbel, "I was coached for three years in high school and two years at Texas Tech by Joe Kerbel. He was the best football instructor I have ever known. He drilled us over and over until the knowledge and execution was second nature. His workouts were always very strenuous and sometimes controversial, but we were always ready to play when game time came around. Many of his players received scholarships because he taught them how to be good at their position and to have the discipline necessary to be a good player. He made it easy for his players to transition into the college level football programs. I have heard many former Joe Kerbel players relate how their coaches, including Bear Bryant, commented how well-coached the Amarillo players were compared to the average high school player. In his three years at Amarillo High, I'm guessing that he helped over 60 players get four year scholarships. Not only that, I know of several student trainers and equipment managers that he helped get scholarships."

I asked him about the most significant district game he played in. He replied, "Personally, the district game that stands out most in my mind was in 1956 against Borger. We were undefeated in district play with Borger and Amarillo Palo Duro left to play. The previous week, Borger had played Palo Duro and beat them by having their backside defensive end tackle the quarterback on every single play. This was a surprise tactic and Palo Duro could never get their offense going. Our coaches had us ready for this. We mainly used the end trap right up the middle, beating the Bulldogs 47-7. I remember several times pointing out to the defensive end who had just tackled me without the ball, that we had scored on the play. This set us up for a historic 27-7 win the next week over Palo Duro in the first game ever played between the two schools, wrapping up the district title for the Sandies." He continued talking about the playoff games, "The most significant playoff game had to be our 33-14 loss to the Abilene Eagles in the Quarter-Finals in 1957. We were both undefeated and Amarillo was favored although Abilene was the defending state champion. There are always excuses, but we were just outplayed and outscored in this game. Nothing we tried would work. It was a very frustrating afternoon for us Sandies."

He had one more anecdote to close out his interview. He spoke of his first year as a sophomore quarterback on the '55 Sandies, "One significant district game we played was in 1955 against the Abilene Eagles in Abilene. This was Joe Kerbel's first year at Amarillo High and Abilene was heavily favored as they were defending state champions with a lot of returning players. I was starting on defense and I was the backup QB. Our starting QB was noticeably very nervous about this big game against the state champions and was having trouble concentrating. As a result, he hadn't looked very good in practice and I. who was not worried about playing QB, was doing everything correctly. The day before the game, Coach Kerbel announced that I would be the starting quarterback for the game. Being a sophomore, playing QB against the mighty Abilene Eagles scared me silly and I didn't get much sleep. Just before the kickoff, Coach Kerbel pulled the other QB aside and said, 'Soapy is a sophomore and a little nervous, so I want you to start the game and I will send him in after a few plays, when he settles down.' The other QB who had gotten a full night's sleep played very well and I never got in to play QB. It was very obvious he never intended for me to start and was a good example of Joe Kerbel's coaching prowess. In the middle of the third quarter, we trailed Abilene 14-13, but then we ran out of gas and lost 35-13, but Abilene had to play their starting team for nearly the whole game."

I mentioned that Soapy might be one of the most visible Sandies ever because of his continuing involvement with Amarillo High as a volunteer. He enumerated that involvement, "I am on a committee to select the winner of the ONCE A SANDIE, ALWAYS A SANDIE scholarship offered by the former players to a player on the team that best exemplifies the Sandie Spirit and is likely to play a role as an alumni in the support of Sandie football. I donate regularly to the Sandie Football and Baseball Booster Clubs and do whatever I can to help the coaches." In his business as a realtor, he sold current Sandie coach Mel Maxfield his home. There is a beautiful black granite memorial monument to former Sandies who perished in wars in which the United States fought that sits on the grounds of an interior patio at the school. Sudbury played a major role in bringing that monument to Amarillo High

As I mentioned earlier, Larry Dippel became the Sandies' head coach in 1975 after a successful four years at Hereford High School. He would be there for 31 years before retiring in 2006 with a 224-119-5 record at the helm of the Sandies. In 1990, he led the Sandies to a 11-3 record and their first Quarter-Final appearance since the '57 juggernaut coached by Kerbel. Two years later, the Sandies made it to the Semi-Finals before losing to the Temple Wildcats coached by Bob McQueen. In an interview in late June 2014, Dippel reflected on his long run at AHS and what it meant to him, some of the games that were especially meaningful to him and a bunch of the Sandie players who stood out to him for their play.

He began, "Amarillo High is a very special place because of their tradition, not only because of their athletic accomplishments, but their entire programs. Their alumni have maintained their school pride and loyalty to their school.

With their loyal support they expected a quality and successful program. They were appreciative and supportive when that was delivered."

He discussed a number of games spread over 24 years that stood out to him as milestone games for the Sandies. He began, "The 9-0 win over Permian in 1979 was the Panthers' first non-district loss in Barrett Stadium." That was their home field in Odessa. He continued, "In 1985, we beat Palo Duro 10-7. Both teams were undefeated playing for the district championship. There were 20.000 fans at Dick Bivins Stadium which had a normal capacity of 15.000 fans. We kicked the field goal on the last play of the game. Palo Duro was leading on penetrations; we had to score to win the game."

End of the game finishes that left the Sandies victorious were the rest of the games that Dippel recalled in this interview."In 2003, we had a goal line stand against Monterey to win 17-13 on the last play of the game. In 1999, we beat San Angelo Central 10-3 in San Angelo, but had to make a goal line stand at the end of the game. In our 1992 Semi-Final run, we had several exciting wins. We came from behind Abilene Cooper to win 20-17 in Bi-District. In the Regional game against Fort Worth Dunbar, we had to make a last minute drive to score at the end for a 21-20 win. Then in the Quarter-Finals, we beat Permian 10-7 in the snow for one of their first Quarter-Final losses. They had defeated us in the third game 26-14. Our free safety intercepted a pass in the end zone on their final possession."

Then he enumerated the players that stood out for their play through the seasons. A couple of them have their own interviews later in the chapter. The first player Dippel cited was Carl Birdsong. He was the rare Sandie player who Dippel allowed to play on both sides of the ball. Birdsong was a wide receiver, defensive back, kicker and punter for the 1975 and 1976 teams. Of course, he is best known for the years he was the punter for the St. Louis Cardinals in the NFL. His comments about being a Sandie follow Dippel's recollections of his players. The next player Dippel mentioned was Mark Mathiasmier, the leading rusher from his fullback spot for the Sandies for three years in 1978-79-80. He was the leading rusher in Class 5A in all of Texas in 1980 with 1445 yards gained. He played later at the University of New Mexico.

In 1997 and '98, Johnny Johnson was the leading rusher both years. Dippel commented, "He was the best all around in that he was a good pass receiver, a great pass protector and returned punts and kickoffs. At times, we would use him to cover kickoffs." He considered Len Wright at center to be the best offensive lineman for his play in 1983 and 1984. He found him to be strong, athletic and intelligent. Wright went on to be All-SWC at Texas Tech. Tackle Sterling Elza from the '91 and '92 Sandies also drew that description of strong, athletic and intelligent. Elza went on to play for Rice. His comments about his time playing for the Sandies are also in this chapter.

Speedy Todd Ringo at safety for the Sandies in 1985 and 1986 was described by Dippel as being fast, smart and a very physical player. Dippel remarked, "With Ringo on the field for two years, the longest run against Amarillo was only 39 yards." Other defensive linemen were Rick Knapp at a defensive end position that now is called the outside linebacker slot in 1975 and 1976, defensive end Clay Stapp whose injury that kept him out of the Semi-Final game against Temple tilted the game in favor of the Wildcats and Chris Jackson, the nose guard on the 1984 and 1985 teams. Dippel mentioned one final player who was one of the rare two way starters for the Sandies, David Scott, the 1983 nose guard and offensive guard. He said, "Scott was very talented. He made All-State both ways. Of the group of defensive linemen, he concluded, "All played extremely hard, all of them were outstanding technicians playing with great leverage making them extremely difficult to block."

Birdsong, as stated, was a two way player for the Sandies in 1975-76. He was first and foremost a punter and kicker, but also a defensive back and wide receiver. The Sandies made it to Bi-District each of his two years on the varsity. He made All-District, Super Team and All-State his senior year. He went on to play on scholarship at West Texas A & M and Southwestern Oklahoma State University. He was drafted by the St. Louis Cardinals of the NFL and was their punter for five years, 1981-85. He picked up a degree in pharmacy. Today, he is back in Amarillo as the president and chief compliance officer of Maxor National Pharmacy LLC. When asked what factors about playing for the Sandies made for special experiences, Birdsong replied, "The Amarillo –Tascosa rivalry, the pep rallies and the media support." He commented about playing for Coach Dippel, "It was a great experience playing for Larry Dippel. He and his staff were very good at coaching details, techniques and creating a positive atmosphere which incentivized the players to want to play harder and create a tradition."

Birdsong talked about several games that stood out to him, "In 1976, we played Pampa for the district championship. I had been sick all week and could not practice. It was extremely cold and by half it was snowing and ended with four inches of snow on the ground. I kicked a 37 yard field goal, played defense and we won 18-0. We met the Monterey Plainsmen for Bi-District after that. Monterey was 10-0 and we had ended 8-2. It was a very hard fought game. We were leading at the half by a field goal I had kicked. Perry Williams, our running back, in the first half ran a sweep and a Monterey defender attempted a tackle, but Perry spun around and sat down on top of him, got up and scored. But the referees inadvertently blew the play dead which was ultimately the difference in the game as Monterey scored in the fourth quarter on a pass from Ron Reed to David Patterson to take a 7-3 lead. We drove the ball to inside the Monterey 30, but we turned the ball over and the game ended 7-3. Monterey went all the way to the Semi-Finals that year."

He has never forgotten his Amariilo roots and discussed ways in which he continued to contribute to the Sandies after he graduated in 1977, "During my career with the Cardinals, the Sandie coaches wanted me to do a punting coaching video which they maintain in the coaching films. I have worked with many high school punters in the area. I have spoken at coaching seminars. Many of the old players still attend the games to watch the current Sandie teams. The Olde Gold bunch (an organization of former Sandie players) talk to the teams when asked by the coaches and we participate in the selection of the ONCE A SANDIE, ALWAYS A SANDIE award."

Sterling Elza came along 15 years after Birdsong and anchored the offensive line at both guard and tackle during the 1990, 1991 and 1992 seasons. In his sophomore year, the Sandies made it back to the Quarter-Finals for the first time since 1957. Then in his senior year, Amarillo played Temple in the State Semi-Final game for the 5A, Division II championship. He was an All-District and Offensive MVP in his senior year. He was an Honorable Mention All-American for Scholastic Coach. Elza played for Rice University. Today, he is a lawyer in Fort Worth, Texas.

Elza responded to questions about his entire football experience at Amarillo High with profound statements that illustrate just how special it was to him to be a Sandie coached by Larry Dippel. He began talking about the community feeling that he felt as he said, "Community with our teammates and with the city of Amarillo and the Panhandle of Texas. Most of the 1992 team had played sports against and with each other since kindergarten. We were all great friends. We all played for each other and were in it together. Like any team, we had injuries. We lost our senior quarterback to injury and he was the biggest supporter of Brent Leather, his junior replacement. Everybody contributed to that season."

He added, "Amarillo High students, parents and graduates have always supported the Sandies. We had great crowds at every home game and always had great representation at away games as well. However as we continued to advance in the playoffs in 1992, the entire city began to back us. It didn't matter if they were from Caprock, Palo Duro or Tascosa. Television, radio and newspapers were all very supportive with special advertising and messages supporting the Sandies. Eventually the entire Panhandle joined in. As we drove to our final playoff game, people in Memphis and all of the communities along

U.S. 287 came out to the highway to show their support with signs and shouts of encouragement as our buses passed through with local police escorts. The entire Panhandle of Texas had rallied behind our team."

About Dippel, Elza commented, "Coach Larry Dippel is one of the best coaches I ever had and was the most even-keeled coach I ever played for. He never got rattled and always seemed to know what to do. His quiet confidence gave the players confidence. I had been playing tight end and defensive line as a freshman. Halfway through spring practice, Coach Dippel grabbed and told me that, due to a couple of injuries, I would be moving to offensive line and would be starting the Varsity spring game. His belief in me throughout my years at AHS both reassured me and drove me to succeed. Coach Dippel and his staff got the most out of each of us and never put us on the field without the game plan and the tools to win. Coach Dippel's excellence as a coach and as a man can be seen in the loyalty that his assistants had for him. Coaches Naril, Cobb, Nash, Bain, Jones and Langdon, among many others stayed with Dippel for years and years when I am sure they had opportunities to be head coaches elsewhere."

Elza then talked about the games of the 1992 season beginning with the district, "In 1992, Amarillo High, Palo Duro and Tascosa all made the playoffs in 3-5A. Palo Duro and Tascosa were both very good teams. We had grown up playing football with and against all these guys since fourth grade. It was very important to all of us to win those games. The district game against Tascosa ended up being the most significant district game that season. They were right in the middle of district schedule. Amarillo High/Tascosa has always been a huge rivalry game. We were undefeated in district, having only lost a non-district game to Permian. Tascosa had some great players including future Olympics gold medalist wrestler, Brandon Slay and future OSU Cowboy Derek Leinin. It was a tough game that we pulled out 14-7. We scored the winning touchdown on a 50 yard pass with two minutes left in the game. While we had been tested during the season, beating Tascosa was a big step towards our goal of going undefeated in district and advancing through the state playoffs." Moving on to the playoffs, he said, "Beating Abilene Cooper in the Bi-District game 20-17 was important as Amarillo teams always seemed to have their playoffs ended by District 4-5A. The 21-20 comeback win against Fort Worth Dunbar for the Regional title may have been the most exciting game I played in high school. We drove 65 yards and scored the winning touchdown with about 10 seconds left on the clock. However the most significant game was the Quarter-Final win over Odessa Permian in the snow at Jones Stadium in Lubbock. Permian was the defending the state champs. We had played them at Ratliff early in the season and lost 26-14. I felt we had missed a chance to beat them with two turnovers inside their 10 yard line. After the game, my offensive line coach, George Cobb and I got together and started discussing how we were going to beat them if and when we saw them in the playoffs. We weren't alone. It seemed everyone on the team was looking forward to a rematch. Permian owned a long winning streak over Amarillo High, including the three times that I had played against them. We had to bus to Lubbock a day early due to a snow/ice storm moving into the area. It was a tough game against a really good Permian team that included a great middle linebacker named Michael Connor, who would go on to success at UTEP. We finally broke through on a trap play up the middle, in which our fullback, Shane Ward went 51 yards for the score. Clay Stapp and our defense held Permian to one score and we had our win over the defending champs. It was a big win for the team and the city. Coach Dippel and his staff had us prepared and confident that we would win. While we knew that the win was significant, it wasn't until later that I realized how much. When I reported to fall camp at Rice University, all my new Rice teammates wanted to know one thing about me: What was it like to beat Permian in the state playoffs?"

Coach Mel Maxfield is beginning his fifth year coaching the Sandies in 2014. In his first four years from 2010 through 2013, the Sandies compiled records of 8-3, 8-4, 10-3 and 7-6. Overall Melfield is 33-16 with the Sandies. He is beginning his 28th year as a Texas high school coach. An advocate of the Wing T formation, he has used it build a 207-100-1 career mark. In the past two seasons, he led Amarillo to the third round of the state playoffs in Class 4A, Division I where Denton Guyer beat them both times enroute to two consecutive state championships. With the realignment by the UIL, the Sandies are in District II of the new Class 6A. Maxfield reflected on what was special about coaching at Amarillo High, "The tradition of the Golden Sandstorm and the positive expectations that the AHS community represents. Football is important to folks within the Sandie community and thus we have tremendous support that motivates our players to give their best effort on a weekly basis. Each year our team goal is to earn a place on our play-off board that is on our high school field that we look at every day. AHS is a special place that has produced some very good football. It's our mission to see that we continue this tradition."

He went on to talk about some of the most exciting wins he had coached the Sandies to, "We've experienced several exciting wins—2010-17-3 versus Tascosa for the district championship—2011-35-21 Bi-District win versus El Paso Americus—2012—35-28 in overtime versus Randall that led to the district title—2013-42-35 win versus El Paso Chapin in the Area round." He cited the 2010 Tascosa game and the 2012 Randall game as the two biggest district games he's coached at Amarillo. He says about the most significant playoff games, "We played the eventual state champion Denton Guyer in both 2012 and 2013 in the third round. We had a great game in 2012 although we came up short 38-30—in 2013, Guyer was by far the better team."

Maxfield talked about the top players he has coached on the Sandies, "We've had many players that contributed to our success, but during my time at AHS, I would have to say quarterback Gabe Rodriguez is at the top of the list. He was a three year starter for us and led us to two district championships and the play-offs all three years he was our QB. Gabe was a great leader who always put the team's success over personal statistics. His attitude had a very positive influence on our team. His last two years, he threw for 34 touchdowns versus only three interceptions. Gabe set school passing records at McMurray as a true freshman." Asked who his pick was on defense, Maxfield quickly replied,"James Castleman. He was the District MVP for two years and garnered All-State honors as well. James is a very gifted athlete who also is AHS's all time leading scorer in basketball. He was a state qualifier in the shot put as well. He could dominate the game defensively with his physical and athletic play. James is very dedicated and a great young man. James is currently finishing up his successful collegiate career at Oklahoma State where he will be a three year starter."

His comments about Castleman inspired me to contact him before he headed back to Stillwater for his senior year and get his thoughts about playing for the Sandies. Castleman commented, " I loved the environment that Amarillo brought to the game. It seemed like it was a custom to play football. In a way it felt as if we honored Amarillo by playing the sport." In addition to having Maxfield as a coach, Castleman started his Sandie career under the tutelage of Brad Thiessen for his first two of three seasons at AHS. About his two coaches, Castleman said, "My first coach was Brad Thiessen, and he did a great job keeping the team together working as one, also he was good at helping athletes excel and become great at their positions. My other coach was Mel Maxfield, and I think having him as a coach was great because he was very similar to Coach Thiessen by bringing the team together, he is also good at helping athletes find their special qualities and helping them get better at them."

Castleman talked about some of the big games in his career at Amarillo beginning with a key game his junior year in 2008, "This would have to be our rival game against Tascosa High. I was never much of a trash talker, but that's all I would hear that game. Players on my team talking trash to their team and them talking trash to us. I always loved this game because it was our rival game. It would be to see who would have bragging rights for the upcoming year. On top of all that we ended up winning the game (AHS- 40, THS-27) and the one play that I remember is when I blocked through the line and blocked a field goal." He continued, "In my last game (as a Sandie) against El Paso Montwood, it was a close game the whole night, but they were up a touchdown. The one play I remember was when I came through and blocked a punt into the end zone where we landed on the ball and scored. But it was called back and we ended the game with them winning." Montwood 19, Sandies 14 to win Bi-District.

I got back to Coach Maxfield to ask about the 2014 season. He commented, "Our goals have not changed for 2014. Our aim is to win district and play into December. It will be a challenge to achieve these goals, but I am confident in our players' desire and the willingness to work to achieve these goals. We have some experience back from 2013 and we feel good about several areas of our team. We were very successful offensively in '13, but struggled some on the defensive side. Our players are ready to improve in that area and I am confident in their efforts to get back where we need to be."

THE BROWNWOOD LIONS

FIRST YEAR THEY PLAYED: 1907
ALL TIME RECORD THROUGH 2013: 702-353-33
PERCENTAGE: 65.95%
PLAYOFF APPEARANCES: 40
STATE CHAMPIONSHIP GAMES WON: 1960, 1965, 1967, 1969, 1970, 1978, 1981
STATE CHAMPIONSHIP GAMES LOST: 1977, 1999

On April 28, 2012, I discovered the Texas version of the Kevin Bacon game in Brownwood. You remember the Kevin Bacon game don't you? It also is called by the premise on which it operates. That there is no more than six degrees of separation between Kevin Bacon and any other actor or actress from any other era of Hollywood. You pick one, say Jane Russell from the 1940s and start figuring out who were her co-stars in particular movies and trace one to another film maybe a few years later in which there is another star who connects via another movie to someone else in an even later film and so until you have connected back to the final actor having been in a film with Kevin Bacon. It took no more than the six movies maximum to connect Jane Russell to Kevin Bacon.

So what is the Texas version of the Kevin Bacon game? As I felt that day while meeting people who were in town at the Gordon Wood Hall of Champions Museum prior to attending the Gordon Wood Hall of Champions Banquet, the Texas version was Brownwood Lion football. It seemed that every coach I met or heard about that day from other high schools had some connection to the Brownwood Lions. And most of the time, it wasn't necessary to go out all six degrees to make that connection. The Kevin Bacon game lives in Brownwood in the form of Lions football connected through the coaches to virtually every other 11 man program of consequence in Texas high school football.

Since I mentioned being at the Gordon Wood Hall of Champions Museum, I will describe what a unique place it is before I write about the man himself. If there is a bucket list for Texas high school football devotees, then two of the items on the list should be a trip to Brownwood to tour this museum and then a trip to Cuero to see its football museum. More about the Cuero museum in its chapter. The Gordon Wood Hall of Champions is located on the second floor of the historic Harvey House Building at 600 E. Depot Street.

The intent of the museum is to honor Coach Gordon Wood for his championship service and the winning spirit exemplified in his protégée. He donated most of his football memorabilia as a monument to the winning spirit that makes champions. A quick mention of the items a football fan will see in it includes a reconstructed locker room with benches, lockers, chalk board and Lion mural. Each of the lockers are outfitted with testimonials to Coach Wood in the form of audio presentations by famous college football coaches who were impacted by or impressed by Wood in one way or the other. Supporters of the museum paid $500.00 each to have the messages created by their favorite college coaches. The messages are accessed by pushing a button labeled with the name of the coach, two to a locker. Among the coaches are Bum Phillips, Darrell Royal, Grant Teaff, Spike Dykes, Barry Switzer, Jimmy Johnson, Bill Yoeman, R.C. Slocum, Hayden Fry, Bobby Bowden, Mack Brown, Gene Stallings, Emory Bellard, Frank Broyles and Bill Parcels. Beloved sports writer and Texas Football Magazine founder and editor David Campbell is also on one of the two to three minutes audio recordings.

A chalkboard with X's and O's is in the room. A display case shows off a scouting report prepared by Coach Kenneth West that depicts how thoroughly Wood and his assistant coaches prepared the players week by week for the games. On another wall is a very meticulous hand written letter by Wood dated July 29, 1985 for each player to remind them what they needed to do to prepare for the upcoming season. The letter is three pages long and contains not only football related instructions on things such as physical conditioning, but also life lessons. There is much more including photos of past players and coaches voted into the Hall of Fame. The inductions began in 2000 and typically have five individuals voted into the Hall each year.

Tours are available from 9:00 a.m until 4:00 p.m. Monday through Friday. Contact the Brownwood Chamber of Commerce at 325-646-9535 or go to the Chamber website to arrange a tour. There is no cost to make the tour, but donations are accepted and appreciated.

But until Gordon Wood became the coach in 1960, the legacy of Lion football was practically non-existent. In 53 years before then, Brownwood had only one district championship and quickly exited the playoffs in Bi-District. That was the 1953 team that finished 9-2. Only two other teams won as many as nine games, in 1945 and 1951. Wood arrived in Brownwood with solid coaching credentials earned at Stamford as he led the Bulldogs to the 1955 and 1956 Class 2A State Championships with 15-0 records each year. Following those title years, he stayed there two more years and then two years at Victoria before making the move in 1960 to head up the Lions. Grabbing the Class 3A State Championship in that first year of 1960 set the stage for a 26 year run by Wood as Brownwood's most beloved coach. When he finally stepped down after a 44 year coaching career in 1985, he had won 394 games and nine state championships. Brownwood was the biggest beneficiary of his coaching prowess. The Lions won district 15 times and state seven times during his tenure. His record at Brownwood was 256-54-7.

One trait that Coach Wood brought out in the men he hired to be his assistant coaches was loyalty. Perhaps the one coach that best epitomized loyalty was Ken West. He was an assistant preparing scouting reports for the upcoming opponents. He spent 22 years coaching the Lions retiring in 1984 from those duties. He became the principal at Brownwood High after that. West retired from the school district and made Brownwood his home afterward for him and his wife Shirley. She passed away in 2013. He commented on what made Brownwood such a special place for him and his family, "The success that we accomplished in the 22 years that I coached is what made it so special to me and my family there at Brownwood. My son Glen was 18 months old when we moved to Brownwood and he was privileged to grow up attending all my football practices every day thus teaching him all the true values of being a team player and team athletics. With that, Glen when he grew up became an active member of the team in 1978 when we won our fifth State Championship."

He answered about his most exciting game he coached, "I would have to say that the Bay City/Brownwood State Semi-Final of '78 was the most exciting game to me when we rebounded from a 10 point deficit with five minutes to go. (The Lions won 33-28). Then the following week we defeated Gainesville 21-12 for the 4A State Championship." He added that as far as district games go, the 1967 game with Wichita Falls Hirschi was the biggest one that he coached in. It ended in a 21-21 tie and Brownwood won on penetrations. I asked him which playoff game was the biggest in which he had coached and he answered, "I would have to say that the 1981 State Championship game against Fort Bend Willow Ridge was the biggest one I have ever coached." Brownwood won the

4A championship 24-9. West closed by giving his thoughts on the individual players versus the teams they played on, "There is not any one player that I can remember that truly stands out. We always considered the team efforts and not individual efforts to be of utmost importance."

Brownwood has had its share of great players that Wood coached, but there is no doubt that the best quarterback he ever coached was Jimmy Carmichael. He was on the Lion varsity for three years in 1967, 1968 and 1969. With him taking the snaps, the Lions won state in 1967 and 1969 and a district championship in 1968. The team had 34 wins and 16 losses for a 68% winning percentage for the Carmichael years. The honors came his way in abundance. He was a second team All-District defensive back in 1967. In 1968, he was All-District quarterback and Honorable Mention All-State. In his senior year, Carmichael garnered five awards; All-District, All Big Country, All-State (3A), Parade All-American, Amarillo Globe News MVP for all classes in Texas high school ball, #1 Blue Chip recruit. Since then as shown in my chapter on Recognition, he has been inducted into the Texas High School Football Hall of Fame and perhaps, the most meaningful honor of all, induction into the Gordon Wood Hall of Champions. All those honors his senior year because of his accomplishments on the field earned him a scholarship to play football for Texas Tech.

He talked about his days at Brownwood High and what it meant to him and his teammates to be Lions. "I grew up in a relatively small town and had the privilege of playing for a team that had an established and yet still growing reputation as a very quality football program. The team had won State Championships in 1960 and 1965 prior to my sophomore year of 1967. Because of the success of the program, the entire community embraced the football team. The most listened to radio program in town was the weekly address given by Coach Gordon Wood, and for away games, the town emptied out to travel and support our team. It was a very special time. But as Glen West (Coach at Brenham H.S.) stated a couple of years ago, 'It wasn't that we thought we were special, but we knew that we were lucky to be part of something special.'"

About Coach Wood, Carmichael commented, "I had the incredible honor of playing all three years of my varsity experience for the best coaching staff ever assembled in the history of Texas high school football. Coach Gordon Wood, Coach Morris Southall and Coach Kenneth West comprised the entire varsity coaching staff and were supported by Coach Don Martin and Coach Royce Blackburn. These were incredible men as well as being incredible coaches. They were well-respected men of honor, who constantly stressed good citizenship ahead of football. Faith, family and football and in that order. While I certainly learned many things about football from these gentlemen, I believe that I learned far more about life from them. They walked the walk and their influence on my life is invaluable."

He continued on about important district games and playoff games he was a part of, "The most significant district game of my career was the 1969 (my Sr. yr) game at Stephenville. Going into that game, our record was two wins and three losses. We had lost to the #1 4A team (Dallas Woodrow Wilson), the #2 4A team (Abilene Copper) and the #8 4A team (Abilene High) and even some of our most ardent fans in Brownwood began to think about how we could finish the season. We were a very down and somewhat beaten up team that traveled to Stephenville. They were very enthusiastic and were ready to play a down Brownwood team. While we didn't play our best game of the season, we did come from behind late in the fourth quarter to win 13-8. On top of that, their frustrations led to a late fourth quarter bench clearing brawl between the teams. Somehow, that victory and the extracurricular activities brought us together as a team, and lifted us back up so that we could win the next eight games and win the State Championship. The most significant playoff game was certainly the Bi-District game in 1969 (my Sr. yr,) versus Lubbock Estacado in Abilene. Going into that game, the new (their second year of varsity play) football team for Estacado was undefeated. They had won the State Championship the previous year and along the path, they beat us 49-8 which stood as the worst loss a Gordon Wood coached team had ever experienced. Estacado was ranked #1 in 3A and was heavily favored to repeat as State Champions. Only through the exceptional efforts of our coaches were we able to summon up the strength and confidence to think that we could beat such a formidable foe. Not only did we give Estacado their first ever varsity loss, we beat them convincingly (29-13). To this day, I am not certain how we were able to pull this victory off. But I do believe that we would have not been able to do this without the best coaching staff in the state."

As is the case with many other former players on teams featured in Friday's Winners, Carmichael stays connected to the Lion football program and legacy, "Currently I proudly serve on the Board of the Gordon Wood Hall of Champions in Brownwood. Coach Wood set this Hall up prior to his passing and we work hard to continue to promote the legacy of this great man. Each year we induct four or five deserving players into the Hall and we make certain that most, if not all, of the current Brownwood varsity football team members have a prominent place in the event. As you can probably tell, I have so much appreciation for the opportunity that I had to be a part of something so very special. As I have gone through my adult years, I often hear from friends that tell of their terrible experiences in playing high school football. I know that I was simply blessed to have been where I was and when I was to play for Brownwood High School and the unique coaching staff that led the program."

For five years between 1986 and 1990, Randy Allen coached the Lions. He followed Gordon Wood, no small task to come immediately after the man who is the legend in Brownwood. Yet Allen held his own with three district championships and one zone championship during his time there. His record with the Lions was 43-13-2. He commented on his stay at Brownwood in the following interview.

"Coach Gordon Wood was highly respected as the winningest coach with the most state championships. He impacted the lives of hundreds of his players. Some of those players lived in Brownwood and their sons played for me. His legacy of great football made coaching in Brownwood special. Coach Wood introduced me to his friends and did his best to lower expectations the first year I coached in Brownwood. He said we would be lucky to be 5-5. We won nine games that first year and the community considered it a successful season."

"Brownwood was special because of the great people of character. I met some of the finest people while coaching there. The school administration was great to me while I coached in Brownwood. Coach Kenneth West was the principal at Brownwood High School. He mentored me and helped me as a coach because he had coached with Coach Wood and been a part of many State Championships."

The players were special and worked very hard to continue the great tradition. The players and coaches were some of the best people I've been around. They were loyal and worked very hard to make the team successful."

Allen discussed the games he coached, "Brownwood had not beaten Cleburne in years. We won the Cleburne game in my first year at Brownwood. (The Lions had last beaten Cleburne in 1981. They ended the four game losing streak with a 14-10 win.) In the playoffs, we defeated Wichita Falls Hirschi using a trick play called the Bell Burn." The Lions beat Hirschi 10-6 in the 1987 Bi-District game.

Mitch Stephens played quarterback and cornerback for the Lions in 2009, 2010, 2011. He was profiled in the Football, a Family Tradition as the third generation of the Croft family. The Lions had three playoff runs while he was there. Stephens started some games as a sophomore, had a torn ACL injury that ended his first year early. He started some more games at QB his senior year. The 2009 team won 10 and lost three, ending the season in the Regional game. The Lions beat Dalhart 33-7 in Bi-District and Seminole 41-28 in Area. Wimberley won the Regional game 24-17. The next year was the best with Brownwood going all the way with 14 straight wins before losing in the State Semi-Finals. The Lions scored a breath-taking 801 points in their 15 game season, an average of 53.4 points per game. Perhaps the first playoff game result served notice to the rest of Class 3A schools that the Lions were for real. In Bi-District, they pulverized Iowa Park 88-24. The next week was nearly as prolific as they ganged up on Bridgeport 61-31 in the Area. In the Regional, the Lions' scoring pace dropped off slightly as they pounded Borger 35-6. Monahans fell 44-16 in the Quarter-Finals. The Brownwood express got derailed in the Semi-Finals by Carthage 35-28. The game results came down to the last play in the game. The 2011 team had an 8-5 record losing in the Regional game to revenge-seeking Monahans 24-13.

The coach was Bob Shipley during those years and the 2012 season, He had his son, Jaxon on the team as a top wide receiver. In 2009, Jaxon had 65 catches for 934 yards and nine touchdowns. In 2010, he got his fair share of that 801 point scoring splurge as he gathered in 87 passes for 1653 yards and 27 touchdowns. That's a two year total of 152 receptions for 2587 yards and 36 scores.

Mitchell commented about what it meant to play at Brownwood. He said, "Playing football in Brownwood is unlike playing anywhere else because there is so much tradition in the football program. Ever since I was little watching from the stands, you always dream of running out of the tunnel to *Welcome to the Jungle* by Guns and Roses. Being a player there you have so much to prove because everybody in the town knows your name, it is almost like you're a celebrity. It is awesome because all of the little kids look up to you."

He continued talking about playing for Coach Shipley, "It was an amazing experience to play for Coach Shipley because he knew all about the game. Most importantly, he was a very religious man and he carried that on and off the field. With his son on the team and me being good friends with his daughter Addie Jane Shipley, most of us players would be at his house hanging out and joking around with him. I think that is good to have a coach who will just hang out with his players off the field and away from the game."

He discussed his playing days on the field, "These aren't district games, but there is one game that was very important to me since it was my first start as quarterback on varsity as a sophomore. Since I had all eyes on me, and people were saying that I was too young and too small, it was important for me to go out there and show all those people I had what it took to be a starting quarterback at Brownwood. We won our game against Liberty Hill 34-17 in 2009. My senior year, 2011, we were playing Graham at their place and going in to half time we were losing. And during half time our coaches were not very happy with us and had some choice words with us. But during all that, they had us look at each of our fellow teammates. I can't remember what we said, but in the end we came out and dominated the second half and came out with the win 35-28. This game was important because it's where we started playing as a team and could count on each other, and also brought us closer as teammates which helped us out for the rest of the season. For my 2010 season, I just tell people that when we played, we always played as a team and everyone on the team had a special part to play and we all did our part."

Perhaps the game that drew the most attention while Stephens played and Shipley coached was the 88-24 Bi-District win over the Iowa Park Hawks in 2010. It drew attention because Iowa Park committed a large number of personal fouls (seven) and drew the ire of Coach Shipley who wanted to protect his players from injury. In the Abilene Reporter News edition of November 12, 2010, it was reported that a spearing play by the Hawks brought Shipley out on the field. Shipley was quoted as saying, "There were some late hits. I told their coach if they would stop hitting us late and stuff like that, we'd stop scoring. That didn't happen."

Stephens picked up describing how that game played out, "During the game there was a confrontation between both coaches. They were playing dirty and Coach Shipley hated it because he didn't want any of our players to be injured because of it. And he was without a doubt trying to protect us. Seeing him all fired up like that made everyone on the team all fired up for the second half. He said we would keep scoring and we were down with his plan. So we kept scoring and we didn't want to stop."

The result was that the Lions set an all-time team playoff scoring record for one game and came within a game of making their 10th appearance in a State Championship game.

Chuck Howard coaches the Lions today. His first year as head coach was 2013. Previously he had been on the Brownwood staff since 2009. He began answering my questionnaire with comments about why Brownwood is so special to him and his family. He said, "It is the great tradition of being a Brownwood Lion. It's the great coaches and players that have coached and played in Brownwood. It's the support of the community."

Asked about the most exciting games he has been involved in, Howard reflected, "I can think of a couple. As an assistant coach it would be the Graham game in 2009-we blocked an extra point in the final seconds of the game to win 28-27. In 2010 we beat Stephenville 42-16." He continued, "The biggest district game has been the 2013 Burnet game. We ran a kickoff back 104 yards with seconds left on the clock to win the district opener 36-31. In 2010, we beat a very good Snyder team in Snyder handily. Both teams were undefeated at the time." I asked him about which playoff games stood out to him, "The Area game versus Seminole in 2009-we were down 28-14 at half and won 42-28. I believe it validated us as a playoff contender. The Semi-Final game in 2010 versus Carthage-lost 28-35."

Coach Howard talked about some of the players he has coached that stood out to him, "Jaxon Shipley, receiver, currently playing at UT-the best offensive player I have seen at any level. Graylon Brown, QB, threw for over 4000 yards. He was a fearless competitor and tremendous leader who wanted the ball in his hands when the game was on the line. Currently pitching at Angelo State."

I asked him about defensive players for the Lions that impressed him, "Our defense forced 49 turnovers in 2010. I will mention three players-Derek Longoria, safety-currently playing at SMU. George De la Paz, nose guard. Caden Ellis, linebacker, 3A Defensive Player of the Year in 2010. They played great together as a unit."

Finally, Howard gave his thoughts on how his 2014 team would stack up as the season neared, "I expect to see marked improvement from a 4-7 2013 team. We will start seven underclassmen on offense and eight underclassmen on defense. Senior starters are QB Colt Bertrand, four year starter, Mike Livingston at guard, Ryan Lewis at guard, Dalton Simmons at linebacker, Isaac Sanchez at TE-DE and Trent Carlton at NG. Junior returning lettermen are Hayden Day at TE-DE, Kory Owen at OT and Grant Lewis at LB. A sophomore returning letterman is Connor Howard at receiver.

THE CAMERON YOE YOEMEN

FIRST YEAR THEY PLAYED: 1911
ALL-TIME RECORD THROUGH 2013: 667-332-43
PERCENTAGE: 65.92%
PLAYOFF APPEARANCES: 40
STATE CHAMPIONSHIP GAMES WON: 1981, 2012, 2013
STATE CHAMPIONSHIP GAMES LOST: 2010

Many Texas high schools are named for famous political leaders - state and national, revered state heroes, geographic and geological features, and local civic leaders. In the case of Cameron Yoe High School, it was named for local merchant C.H. Yoe, but under a set of circumstances that makes his name being on the school nameplate one of the most unique tales in Texas history. There is probably no other district in Texas where the students and faculty of that school district are bound by the terms in a will that makes them pay homage to a benefactor every year on a special school holiday - except for those who are in the Cameron ISD.

The Cameron students take pride in their unique celebration that has been carried on every year since 1921. I had wondered for a long time why the school was called Cameron Yoe High School and its teams the Yoemen. When they won 30 of their last 31 games and two state championships in Class 2A-Div I, they had worked their way into the bottom rungs of the teams I was profiling in this book and it gave me the opportunity to research how this came about. Several people tried to explain it to me, but when Rhonda Gelner gave me a link to what 1999 Yoe graduate Denise Schope Mattox had written about the gift and its terms and how she felt about it (a lot of pride), I knew her words were the best way to explain the Yoe mystique. With her permission, here is what she wrote in 2009 on the eve of her 10-year class reunion.

"I attended C.H. Yoe High School in Cameron, Texas. Graduating class of 1999. One of my favorite things about high school was what we simply referred to as 'Yoe Pride'. Before I could even begin to try to explain the concept of Yoe Pride, I need to give a brief history of my high school. Unlike most high schools, we weren't named after our town. We were named after the benefactors whose love for Cameron and the children within it made the high school possible: Charles H. and Caroline Yoe.

After C. H. Yoe passed away, Caroline gave the money to buy the land and build the high school for Cameron, where they had made their home together for so many years. In 1921, it was dedicated and opened in the name of C.H, Yoe High School. Our mascot became a 'Yoeman' —a medieval archer similar to the character of Robin Hood. The original building, built in 1921, still stands, and it's where I had a vast majority of my classes between 1995-1999. In 2004, a new high school was built on the same land.

Since 1921, in May, Cameron ISD takes a school holiday—'Yoe Day'— to remember, thank and honor C. H. and Caroline Yoe. On that day, officers in organizations in the high school and representatives of every class—from seniors through kindergarten enrolled in CISD—come together to hold a memorial ceremony to place flowers on the graves of C.H, Caroline and their daughter, Laura.

I sincerely believe that it is in this memorial, this moment of respect for where our school came from, that Yoe Pride originates. We can claim it to be due to our football team or any academic success we may have. But in the end, our school would not be what it is (and was) if not for the love of one couple for our town almost one hundred years ago."

According to other comments and responses from Denise and others in town, Yoe Day is observed the second Thursday in May each year. The graves of the three Yoes are in the Oak Hill Cemetery. Early on the morning of Yoe Day, the class and organization representatives and officers drive in a funeral-like procession to the cemetery carrying the flowers that are put on the Yoes' graves. Part of the tradition is the reading of Caroline Yoe's will each year, which has the instructions in it for carrying on this unique tradition. When the service ends, a member of the Yoe band plays Taps. Denise says,"I always get a chill down my back when I hear that music performed at the end of this ceremony."

Yoe Pride is measured very easily in the performance of its football teams over the last 102 years. And that is what the rest of this chapter is about. Football is just one aspect of Yoe Pride. Denise lists many of the others in her summary and then closes it with the following words, "And I admit it. I still have it strong today. And I always will." Her words are echoed by many other Yoemen from the earliest years to the classes of today.

That community pride for the Yoemen shows up in the regular attendance at the Booster Club meetings, even when school is nearly out for the year. It shows up in individual acts of volunteerism to enhance the Cameron program. One such individual who continues to do his part year after year is Bertie Shumate. He is beginning his 44th year as the stadium announcer. His brother, Max Shumate, was as passionate as Bertie, recording the key information on all the Cameron games beginning in 1950 until his passing. Max had a series of notebooks that he filled with the dates and game results. Since his passing, Bertie has taken on that duty and has them ready to show someone at a moment's notice.

Mack McKinney came into the Cameron program in the mid 60s. He was a freshman in the 1962 season and graduated in 1966. He played quarterback and safety for the Yoemen. As the starting quarterback his junior year in 1964, he guided the Yoemen to a 6-4-1 record. It was their first time in the playoffs since 1958. In his senior season, Cameron went two rounds deep in the playoffs, for the first time since 1951. For his efforts, McKinney was the All-District quarterback and safety both years. He was chosen All Central Texas his senior year and was selected to play in the Texas High School Coaches Association All-Star game following his graduation from Cameron. He went on to play football for the Texas Longhorns on scholarship.

McKinney discussed the coaches he had at Cameron,"John Roberts was my coach as a freshman. George Kirk coached me the other three years. We had some outstanding assistants who became THSCA HOFers later - Bob McQueen at Temple, John Wilkins at Odessa Permian. Kirk was a THSCA HOFer as well. Ken Fuqua, who took over as head coach when Kirk left after my senior year, was an outstanding coach as well. They were all outstanding teachers of fundamentals, which I felt gave me an advantage over many of my UT teammates from larger schools."

McKinney, who today is a purchasing agent for a large home builder in Austin, reminisced about some of the games that stood out to him, "Our biggest rival was Rockdale, a state finalist my freshman year and went far in the playoffs my sophomore year. They beat us pretty handily both years. We returned the favor the next two years. Our biggest non-district rival was Taylor. My junior year, they beat us handily in the regular season and we almost pulled an upset in Bi-District (12-7) as the Ducks advanced to the State Semi-Finals. My senior year we beat them decisively in both the regular season and Bi-District (33-7) before running into Bellville (34-16) which featured my future Longhorn teammate, Ted Koy and about four or five others who received Division I scholarships."

He commented about the current crops of Yoemen in closing, "Under Coach Rhoades, the Yoemen have been very successful the last few years, so I don't think they need my help."

Cameron won its first State Championship in 1981. Toby York was in his first year as the Yoemen head coach. The team ran up a 13-1-1 record to win the title. In the two years before this achievement, the Yoemen had two other head coaches. Both had 6-4 records, not enough to advance in the playoffs either year. Max Graham coached in 1979, while Jim Smith succeeded him for the 1980 season. We caught up with Jeff Boutwell who played in those three seasons - two so-so years, three different coaches and ultimately a state title. He shared how it was during those years. "The whole town is behind you. When the team traveled, they literally closed the town down. I had three coaches, Max Graham, '79, Jim Smith, '80 and Toby York, '81. The staff under Coach York was very young. It was a different atmosphere than under the other coaches' regimes."

Naturally, his best recollections were of the games played in his senior year when they won state. The non-district game that was the most memorable to Jeff was against Austin Westlake. "We came from 10-0 down at halftime and beat the Chaps 28-10. Coach York came in at halftime and tore up the play sheet and said we were going to run the power sweep from the Wing T until they stopped it. They never stopped it. After that, we felt pretty good about ourselves." The district game was against Hearne, "They were the team to beat. It was for the district championship. They were very athletic and supposedly had the best quarterback that we played against. Toby liked to come up with different challenges every week and that week, it was the QB. We shut him down and won 21-7." He continued, "Our most significant playoff win was the Bi-District game at Yoe Field against Manor. We were down 14-7 late in the game. Toby called the Belly Bum. Oscar Riggins took the ball on the trick play and scored from about 35 yards out. We were behind on penetrations and first down so we had to go for two. We then scored the two point conversion and won 15-14."

Boutwell discussed their advancing further into the state playoffs, "The next most important game was the Quarter-Finals against Newton. They had a nationally ranked running back named Antony Byerly. There were all kinds of college scouts in the stands. Even ABC Sports was there. We jumped out to a big lead at halftime, but Byerly did his thing in the second half. The score was 28-28 with about four minutes left in the game. We were behind on penetrations, but ahead on first downs. It was fourth and four from about the Newton 40 yard line. Toby called a quick pass to Riggins. I was supposed to go out and kick the defensive back out. The play went off. I basically clipped the defensive back and Riggins ran up the field and was hit by their middle linebacker in the thigh. It sounded like a watermelon exploding! Riggins made the first down. We eventually made the penetration and ended up on Newton's one yard line. We didn't know the penetration or the first down count and the team in the huddle was very concerned about kneeling out the clock and the game for three downs. Toby later told us he didn't want Byerly to get his hands on the ball again. We won the game and Byerly went on to play at Texas. We then beat Port Isabel in Victoria in the Semi-Finals. They were bragging about their defense not giving up but 25 points in the whole season. We scored on our first play from scrimmage and never looked back beating them 25-14. Of course, we beat Gilmer 23-3 in Waco at Floyd Casey on a cold December day. I think they had a total of 60 yards of offense."

Another Yoeman from that era is Paul Hoelscher, the quarterback and defensive back from 1980 through 1982. As mentioned in the paragraphs above about Boutwell, the Yoemen didn't make the playoffs in 1980, Hoelscher's sophomore season. They won state in 1981 and ended their season at the state Quarter-Finals in 1982, his senior year. He was a unanimous All-District pick, All-State at both positions and Central Texas Player of the Year in his senior year. He was recruited to play football in college, but chose instead to take a baseball scholarship to the University of Texas.

About being coached by Toby York in his junior and senior years, Hoelscher said,"We were very disciplined in everything we did. Coach Oliver, the defensive coordinator was instrumental in setting the tone in every meeting. I had complete confidence that our scheme would be successful week to week. We were very physical and tried to punish teams offensively and defensively. We played/beat the bigger schools in non-district which prepped us for district and the playoffs."

Then Hoelscher talked about some of the significant games he played in, "My junior and senior year, we had to beat Hearne for the district championship—we were both ranked in the top five. My junior year we won 14-7. My senior year we won 17-14 on a last second field goal by Mariano DeLaRosa. I had one passing touchdown and an interception in the end zone. We drove 82 yards with 1:10 left in the game." In personal achievements, Hoelscher mentioned, "I had two rushing touchdowns in the Semi-Final game. Then I had two passing touchdowns in the State Championship game."

Asked about his involvement in Yoemen football since he graduated, he answered, "I spoke at a few All Sports banquets. Coach Rhoades invited me to speak to the team before the State Championship game in 2012. I loved my teammates—still do. It's like we have always been together when we get together. I had some pretty cool individual accomplishments/experiences in my sports career but the most fun I had was battling with my 'boys' on Friday night."

The Yoemen have been among the hottest teams in Texas the past two years as measured by their 30 wins in 31 games and their two state championships in Class 2A-Division I in 2012 and 2013. They were 15-0 in 2012 and 15-1 in 2013. Their titles were won with victories over Daingerfield 38-20 in 2012 and over Wall 35-14 in 2013. The players were totally committed to achieving these levels and worked very hard to make the wins happen. One of the players on both those teams was outside linebacker/running back/receiver Michael Gelner. He graduated in 2014 as the Cameron valedictorian. That indicates the emphasis that the Yoe puts on all aspects of student life. Another proof of the emphasis is the sign posted on Highway 77 showing that Cameron Yoe won the Lone Star Cup in 2011. The Lone Star Cup is awarded by the UIL to a school in each classification that gathers the most points in all athletic competition, marching band, one-act play and UIL academic competition at the state level.

If there is any one player who personifies what the Yoe tradition in football is, it is Gelner. He explains about the special experience of playing football in Cameron. "Cameron fans love Friday night football and it is a great feeling looking up in the stands and having the support of your town and future Yoemen behind you. I have enjoyed coaching flag football during my reign on Varsity. These future Yoemen look up to the Varsity players and if any way I can make a positive influence on a person that is a great feeling. There is so much tradition at C.H. Yoe High School and that adds to the experience."

Gelner explained how they won back to back state titles as he stated, "In Cameron, we have a winning tradition that goes along with a no quit mentality. A big group of us were at the school working out in the weight room and running throughout the summer. We were determined to win it again." But along the way, the Yoemen's undefeated season went down the tube when district rival Lago Vista snapped their 20 game winning streak with a 27-20 upset. Gelner had his thoughts about what how this loss played into their getting back on track for the drive to defend their state championship, "Whether or not this was the most significant district game, I feel our only season loss to Lago Vista in 2013 was a crucial part of completing our 2013 season. Defensively we didn't play well in this game and offensively they contained us. The loss eventually caused us to share the District title with two others. It mentally prepared us for what was to come. We could be beat. You have to play your game offensively as well as defensively the whole 48 minutes, not just part of the time. The following week we played McGregor and I would have to say that was the most fun I've ever had."

He skipped ahead to the Semi-Final game against top-ranked White Oak. "They had us down by two touchdowns at the half 21-7. I was really emotional and went to the locker room and gave my teammates my own half-time speech before Coach Rhoades came back in to send us out. But we came out hard in the third quarter and defensively shut them out. The score was 24-21 with a little over a minute left in the ball game. White Oak had the ball, threw two completions, and on the third I intercepted the ball to seal the deal. We were headed back to Arlington for the second year in a row."

He concluded his comments speaking of Coach Rick Rhoades, "Words can't explain the experience I have had playing for him. He has a wonderful coaching philosophy and an excellent coaching staff to put it all in motion. He's the only head coach I've played for."

Rhoades is in his sixth season coaching the Yoemen. His Yoe teams from 2009 through 2013 have won 55 of the 66 games they played. All of the coaches of teams in this book were asked the same set of questions to end the chapters written about their school teams individually. Here is what Rhoades responded.

1. What is it about coaching in that school and in that town that makes it so special to you and your family? "The support that we get from our community. Athletics is important in Cameron, Texas, especially football."

2. What has been the most exciting win you have coached at that school? "There have been a couple that have been exciting. First, the Quarter-Final 35-14 over Tatum in 2010. In second was this year's win over White Oak. They were number one in the state as well and we were down 21-7 going into half. We came out and played a great second half and ended up winning the game 24-21. And obviously, the two State Championship games were huge wins, particularly the win over Daingerfield in 2012 (38-20). They defeated us in 2010 (33-27) in a heart breaking game. We tied the game with 47 seconds left and lost it with 26 seconds left. It was great to come back and beat them in 2012."

3. What has been the biggest district game, perhaps with the district championship on the line, that you have coached there to date? "Probably this year's game against McGregor. We had lost the previous week to Lago Vista and McGregor came into our stadium undefeated in district. Our kids came out and played one of the best games we played all year and beat the Bulldogs 55-13."

4. Also, what playoff game has been the biggest one you have coached there? "The Tatum and White Oak games I mentioned earlier."

5. Is there any offensive player you have coached who stands out as the best player you have coached? What makes him that outstanding? "We have had a bunch of players that have stood out offensively: Jack Rhoades (his son) and Jason Kopriva at quarterback. Damyon Kelley, Keaton Denio and Traion

Smith at running back. Cotton Shuffield, Thomas Rinn, Dede Westbrook and Aaron Sims at receiver. Kylen Harrell at offensive guard. All these have been outstanding football players for us."

6. How about a defensive player? "We have had some great ones there as well. Deantana Holt and Edgar Luna were great defensive linemen for us. Somari Wright and O'Neal Spells at inside linebacker. Michael Gelner, Jarrett Beckhusen and Cheyenne Black at outside linebacker. Colt Labay, Jalen White and Treion Sims in the secondary. All of these were great defensive players for us."

7. What do you anticipate for your team for the 2014 season? What are your strengths and weaknesses, returning personnel, etc. for your team? "I think we have a chance to be a really good team. We return three starters on offense and three on defense, so there will be a lot of new faces for us. If some of the new faces come through for us like I think that they can, we could be really good."

THE CORSICANA TIGERS

FIRST YEAR THEY PLAYED: 1905
ALL-TIME RECORD THROUGH 2013: 679-375-44
WINNING PERCENTAGE: 63.82%
PLAY OFF APPEARANCES: 39
STATE CHAMPIONSHIP GAMES WON: 1932, 1963
STATE CHAMPIONSHIP GAMES LOST: 1982, 1997

The arrival of Johnny Pierce as the head coach of the Tigers in 1925 was the start of 16 years of team prosperity, ending after the 1941 season. It was the only head coaching job Pierce ever had. He guided Corsicana to a 124-44-11 record, five district championship, two Semi-Final appearances and the 1932 State Championship over Masonic Home. Corsicana was awarded the championship because the Tigers led in penetrations 3-0 in a game that ended in a 0-0 tie. In my chapter, When Paths Crossed, this would have been a banner year for schools in *Friday's Winners* playing each other based on Corsicana's schedule before the Tigers reached the playoffs. Corsicana blanked Highland Park 20-0 and Tyler 45-0 before polishing off Temple in a close contest 14-12. Had Masonic Home lost their State Semi-Final game, then the Tigers would have met Amarillo High for the State Championship. But the Home prevailed 7-6 over the Sandies to earn the right to come to Corsicana for the State Championship game. With the onset of World War II, Pierce went into the Army as an instructor and died of a heart attack in 1943.

The Tigers went into a drought after that, gaining district championships in 1947 with an 8-2-1 record and in 1949 with a 10-1-0 record as Brad Payne coached them to both Bi-District appearances. Then there was nothing until Jim Acree became the head coach in 1960. He had two years of head coaching experience at Bonham High School in 1958 and 1959. He was 10-1-0 his first year there and 10-2-0 in his second year. He was the right man to take over the

Tiger program after beginning his career with those two district championships. And as Donny Denbow stated in his interview as an All-State player on Corsicana's 1963 state champion team, "Jim Acree was an outstanding motivator. Very demanding and a strong disciplinarian." Acree ran his personal string of consecutive district championships to six in a row as he coached the Tigers to a 7-3-1 record in 1960, 9-2-0 in 1961, 8-3-0 in 1962 and then the 14-0-0 State Champion of Class 3A in 1963. He stayed on to coach for three more years at Corsicana and had a seven year coaching record there of 63 wins, 15 losses and two ties.

Acree's first quarterback on his Tiger teams of 1960 and 1961 was Tom Wilson. He made All-District for his play as both teams he led made it to the Bi-District rounds. The 1961 Tigers won Bi-District, but lost in the Quarter-Finals to Gainesville 38-19. He played well enough to earn a scholarship to play quarterback for Texas Tech in 1964 and 1965. His assessment of Acree very closely matched what Denbow said about the coach who broke Corsicana's string of eleven years of missing the playoffs, "Jim Acree was a strong disciplinarian. He believed that with hard work, you could achieve anything in life. He was truly an outstanding coach."

Denbow got to play only that one year in 1963 because he had a knee injury that kept him from playing his sophomore and junior years. He played as a split end his senior year. As mentioned above, he made first team All-State then. His play was good enough to gain him a full scholarship to SMU. What he noticed about playing for the Tigers was, "The entire town follows the program and are interested in players as individuals." He considered his first district game against Ennis to be the most significant district game in which he played. He commented, "We beat Ennis in that first district game (56-8). I caught two short passes and scored long touchdowns and returned an onside kick for a TD." In the playoffs, he continued, "We met Graham in the Semi-Final game. I scored the first touchdown on a sprint out pass for sixty yards. In our last drive of the game, I caught a pass on the Graham two yard line enabling us to score and successfully go for two to win the game." The Tigers won 14-13.

If Donny Denbow, the player, was special for Corsicana, then move forward fourteen years and see how special Don Denbow, the coach, was for his alma mater. He took over as the head coach in 1977 and stayed for sixteen years coaching the Tigers, retiring from coaching after the end of the 1992 season. His teams compiled a 124-51-10 record with the peak year being 1982 when they played for the State Championship, but lost to Sugarland Willowridge 22-17 at Kyle Field. Denbow spoke about those games, both critical and exciting, and the Corsicana tradition in an interview in late July 2014. I asked just what is it in coaching there that makes it so special for him and his family. He replied, "The tradition started in 1960 when Jim Acree arrived from Bonham and promptly turned the program around. Also before integration, Jackson High School (the black high school) was ultra successful with many State Championships in their classification. Integration was difficult, but the one factor that made students pull together was the football program." About the most exciting game he coached, Denbow said, "It was the 1982 Semi-Final win versus Cleburne, a Chuck Curtis coached team. The score was 7-3 in cold conditions in Texas Stadium." He stated the biggest game he ever coached for the Tigers was the 1982 State Championship game at Kyle Field versus Sugarland Willowridge. But for the most exciting district game, he went back a year and said, "Our 1981 home game versus Ennis. They were rated one or two in the state and were supremely talented. Our players played hard and we were able to win district with that victory." Corsicana prevailed 8-0 in that game.

Denbow replied that the best offensive player he ever coached was, "Bill Jones, a running back who had the blend of power and speed that made him difficult to tackle." Kent Tramel, the noseguard on the 1982 state finalist team drew his nod as the best defensive player he ever coached. Closing with some other thoughts, he said," My son (Don Ashley Denbow) was my QB in 1990 and an All-State punter. His second son, Trevor, will be a sophomore on the 2014 varsity starting at strong safety." To continue promoting the positive aspects of Corsicana football, he says, "We always point to the life-changing experience of playing high school football and working as a team."

One player who bought into Denbow's way of coaching was Richey Cutrer who played two years of varsity ball for the Tigers, 1981 and 1982. He played strong safety, punter and backup quarterback as the Tigers made it to Bi-District in 1981 before going all the way to the State Championship game in 1982. Cutrer got honors as an All-District defensive back and an All-District punter as well as the District Defensive MVP. He walked on at Stephen F. Austin.

I got to know him while he was an assistant coach at Groesbeck High for several years. I covered Groesbeck sports for the Groesbeck Journal and found him to be a great personality with a lot of regard and care for the kids he coached. He was about to return to Corsicana to join the coaching staff when the head coaching/athletic director job at Groesbeck became open and he was hired to stay at Groesbeck. He was there for six years and took the Goats to winning records in his last two seasons, as well in his third year in Groesbeck. His teams had great offensive schemes and he helped six or seven Goats get a chance to play at the next level. Of course, a huge part of his success came from the lessons he had learned as a Corsicana player. He talked about his years as a Tiger player in the following interview.

About the Corsicana tradition and mystique, Cutrer says, "It's the excitement of the community to support the players and the team. They were very supportive and encouraging. At the time, the opportunity to do something that had not been done in nearly twenty years (Make it to the State Championship game). The desire you had as a Tiger to make your mark on the program-leaving an honorable legacy-for others to follow. The chance to have a life experience with guys that you had grown up with that would last forever."

Cutrer talked about being coached by Denbow, "Our head coach was a very discipline-oriented and 'you-did-what-the-coach-told-you-do' type coach. As a player, you didn't listen to outsiders or even your parents when they thought they knew what needed to be done-you learned that from your coaches, because we were the only people at practice, in meetings, in film and out on the field. The experience was a team experience because we were together. Our head coach was a hometown boy who had won a State Championship in high school and that was something that the players looked at as a positive because he was one of us."

Then he discussed some of the district and playoff games that impacted him, "The most significant district game was in 1982 playing Waxahachie. We were both ranked in the top ten in the state, big home game. The best pre-game we had as a team took place that night. We also embarrassed ourselves in front of our home crowd. We lost 24-7 and that was the catalyst for our team to understand what it took to be winners. That defeat was an eye opener and that is what helped us make a run to the State Championship game. Our Semi-Final game against Cleburne was played at Texas Stadium. Cold, rainy and snow through the hole in the roof during pregame. We had two goal line stands that made the difference in the game. We won 7-3."

"Our Bi-District playoff game against Carthage was played in a rainstorm in Longview. Water stood on the field and it rained throughout the game. Carthage had two thousand-yard rushers and the offense was explosive. The weather was called 'Tiger Weather.' No matter the conditions, it was 'Tiger Weather.' That way of thinking played to our advantage that night. Pre-game was difficult for Carthage, tip toeing around the field and doing all they could to not fall on the field and get muddy. As we watched them, the excitement grew and we played to the theme of 'Tiger Weather.' We totally dominated the Carthage offense. Their total offense was less than 50 yards for the game. I had three fumble recoveries." (Corsicana won 32-0.)

Asked what he did to promote the magic of playing Tiger football, Cutrer responded, "I talk about the experience and how special a time it was in my life. Practices during the playoff time of year, playing in big venues and the support that I experienced from the community and school. I share experiences that I had with my team and let the players know how easy it could be the team I am helping coach. I have used motivational things that we used during the season and made it personal for my team. I share pictures of myself, the team and the games we played just to let them see what could be in store for them."

After Denbow retired, Tom Wilson came back to his alma mater as the head coach. After he graduated from Texas Tech, he stayed on there as an assistant coach until 1972. He became the offensive coordinator at Texas A & M in 1975 under Emory Bellard. Coach Bellard resigned as the A & M head coach six games into the 1978 season and Wilson stepped up and coached A & M for the next three and a half years. Then He coached at Palestine High as the head coach for seven years. Denbow retired and Wilson became the head coach of the Tigers from 1993 until retiring after the 1999 season. His Tiger teams compiled a 69-32 record.

The Tigers made the playoffs six years under his guidance. His 1994 team got all the way to the Semi-Finals where they lost to Stephenville 28-6. Three years later, Wilson took them to the next level as they lost in the Class 4A, Division II State Championship game to Texas City 37-34. The game was played at the Astrodome.

He commented about his coming back to Corsicana to coach, "It was my hometown. We had good players, great fans and parent support." Asked about the players who stood out that he coached, Wilson said, "Running back Ketric Sanford was the most outstanding. He had great endurance, toughness, speed and running talent. He was an outstanding team player. The best defensive player I coached was linebacker Gary Jessie. (1993-96) He was smart, a tremendous leader, tough with great instincts." Sanford carried the ball 1058 times for the Tigers during his career. That was the third most carries by any player in all of Texas high school history at the time. He gained 6,762 yards. With the passage of time and constant assaults by today's players on the records, Sanford has moved down to the fifth most career carries in Texas history.

After both playing and coaching at their alma mater, Denbow and Wilson are now members of the Corsicana City Council.

Sanford interviewed with me about his time as a Tiger in late August 2014. He was on the varsity for the seasons of 1993 through 1995 as a running back. With Corsicana making it to Bi-District his sophomore year, the State Semi-Finals his junior year and to the Area finals his senior year and with his big rushing numbers, he drew a lot of post-season honors all three seasons. As a sophomore in 1993, he was first team All-District, District Offensive Newcomer of the Year and All Golden Circle. In 1994, he repeated as first team All-District, District Offensive Player of the Year, District Most Outstanding Player,

All Golden Circle, first team All-State and the 4A Offensive Player of the Year in Texas. It only got bigger and better his senior year. He was the Gatorade Football Player of the Year, first team All-State, District Offensive Player of the Year, District Most Outstanding Player of the Year, first team All-District, All Golden Circle and All-American. He received a scholarship to play for the University of Houston.

What triggered these honors was the way he compiled the yardage rushing each year. He had 253 carries for 1205 yards as a sophomore. In 1994, his junior year, he rushed 475 times for 2,761 yards. In 1995, he rushed 330 times for 2,611 yards. He had one game against Whitehouse his senior year where he gained 376 yards. Since then, one other Tiger running back has had a bigger individual game rushing than Sanford: Lanontra Owens with 457 yards against Sulphur Springs in 2013.

Sanford talked about why he wanted to play ball for the Tigers, "As a kid, it was one of the things I always wanted to do, the thing I always wanted to be a part of. My dad played football and I wanted to be like him. I wanted to be a Tiger. I wanted to play on Friday night. It felt good to be a part of something that had such a tradition; football was/is a big part of the community, to the point that it's ingrained in your DNA to be a Corsicana Tiger."

Then he discussed what it was like having Tom Wilson as his coach, "It was great being coached by Tom Wilson; it was a pleasure and an honor. Coach Wilson genuinely cared about his players. That statement may not be any different from any other coach in high school football, but you knew where you stood with him. We had an unbelievable coaching staff that followed the same mindset. We were family. The other unique thing that he did was in the way that we practiced. Two-a-days were hard and physical; when the season rolled around, the practices were more mental (making sure you knew your assignments). We had to finish runs or plays in practice for added conditioning (we were usually stronger than our opponents in the fourth quarter). It was about giving 100 per cent in everything that we did. Every opportunity could be your only and last chance to prove yourself, to make a difference."

I asked him what district games were most significant and he replied, "That is a tough question. There were many district games that I played were significant, mainly because of the people I played with. I have always been a firm believer that what I did on the field was the direct result of the people I played with. The game that sticks out the most was from my junior year. We were playing Palestine. We were having a good season, and we played a lot of good teams and in the process, we developed our identity as a fast and physical team. The game was a little bizarre; it was literally the game of two halves in that we played the first half on Friday night and the second half the following Saturday afternoon. In the end, we lost. All the momentum that we gained the night before couldn't be recaptured. In that loss, we learned that we had to be better than we were the last game. I've believed that this game was one that changed everything for us that season. Losing that game contributed to the long run we had in the playoffs and will never be forgotten." The game was spread out over two days because of rain storms. Corsicana lost to the Wildcats 21-14.

I followed up asking Ketric the same questions about playoff games. He answered, "The Area game in 1995 against Mount Pleasant. I often look back to that game and think, 'What if? What if I had broken a few of those tackles? What if I had gotten to the outside? What if I...? We had a good team. I believe we were ranked #2 in the state and many picked us to be the State Champions. Mount Pleasant had a good and fast defense and they weren't going to let us beat them, especially with the run. They stopped our running game early and often. We missed a couple of passes in critical situations. Their team made some big plays when they needed them to keep drives going. Ultimately we ran out of time and lost the game (19-3); they earned and deserved every part of their victory against us. After the game, I knew it was my last time to suit up as a Tiger; the last time I would play with the guys that I grew up with for so many years; the last time we would have anything in common. Ending a chapter of our lives together, something we were so proud of."

Asked if he does anything to promote the current teams, he responded, "No, I don't make it back home as often as I would like. But I still follow the team; however I believe that a little of the Corsicana Tiger tradition has gone. When I played for Corsicana all the coaches knew what was required to be a Tiger, the tradition involved. Many of the coaches either played at Corsicana and came back or had been there long enough to understand what the Tiger way meant and represented in the community; that feeling and understanding of Corsicana tradition begins when you're in elementary school, but you start believing it when you put on 'the gold and the blue' for the first time.

Life doesn't always take us where we want to go; it will direct us where we need to go."

Phil Castles coached the Tigers from 2009 through 2012. They finished 6-6 in 2009, 7-4 in 2010, 13-2 in 2011 and 4-7 in 2012. That 2011 team lost to Aledo 68-28 in the Class 4A, DII Semifinal game. In his last season, Castles got the Tigers back to Bi-District where they lost to Red Oak 58-20. Then he left to take over coaching at Henderson.

Stephen Hoffman was a late hire in May 2013 to become the Tigers' new head coach. He came from Del Rio where he got the Rams into the playoffs all seven years from 2007 through 2012. In his best two years of coaching at

Del Rio-2009 and 2012, the team went 10-3 each year. In all, he had a 46-24-0 mark with the Rams. Coming to Corsicana late in the school year meant that he missed out on the spring training session. So he had limited time to get to know his new Tiger team. Corsicana finished with a 2-7 record in 2013. In visiting with him in early August 2014, Hoffman felt like he and his coaching staff would get his team playing in his style that had been successful at Del Rio in the 2014 season.

THE CUERO GOBBLERS

FIRST YEAR THEY PLAYED: 1912
ALL-TIME RECORD THROUGH 2013: 670-355-36
PERCENTAGE: 64.84%
STATE CHAMPIONSHIP GAMES WON: 1973, 1974, 1987
STATE CHAMPIONSHIP GAMES LOST: 1970, 1975, 1985, 1986, 1993, 1998, 2004

In 1919, a group of investors bought a franchise from the new professional football league that was being formed. The group was from Green Bay, Wisconsin. Casting about for a team name, they chose one which reflected a major business in the town. There were at least seven or eight meat packing plants in the little town. In short order they became the Green Bay Packers. What they have accomplished in the National Football League since then is the stuff of legends. Their winning ways make the Packers a team greatly admired and respected by sports fans everywhere. The meat packing business that provided the inspiration for their team name has diminished in the number of plants within the Green Bay city limits. Today only three meat packing plants still ply their trade there.

But in the little south Texas city of Cuero, much of the same type scenario has played out over the decades with its high school football team. Over 100 years ago, the area around Cuero became the center of turkey farming. It was the major industry for several decades. Cuero High School, which began playing football in 1912, perhaps provided an inspiration to the Green Bay investors in choosing a team name related to the meat packing industry around the town. The Cuero team became the Gobblers. The coincidence of Green Bay naming their team by the same source of inspiration was probably not intentional at all, but there is no coincidence that Cuero High School football has achieved great results since it began playing 102 years ago. That is borne out by its record of 670 wins in that span. Also, the Gobblers have appeared in more state championship games than any of the other teams in this book. Their 10 appearances are topped only by Converse Judson of San Antonio, playing in 11 state championships. The Gobblers have made it to the final week in December in UIL play in 1970, 1973, 1974,1975,1985, 1986, 1987,1993, 1998 and 2004. They have three titles to show for their efforts, in 1973, 1974 and 1987.

Getting back to the Packers being named because their owners were motivated by the naming of the Gobblers sounds like a fantasy, given the distance between Texas and Wisconsin, but the Gobblers are definitely known beyond the Texas border. That's illustrated by the story told me by the Gobblers' coach Travis Reeve on June 3, 2014, "Several years ago, a former Gobbler, Anthony Warren, who played in the mid 80s and is now in a mentoring business focusing on NFL players, was in Washington DC to meet with a group of NFL executives. Before the meeting began, the group was engaged in small talk getting to know each other. Warren was asked where he was from. He replied south Texas. They asked where exactly. He said a little town southeast of San Antonio. He was pressed, 'What town', He replied, 'One you've never heard of, Cuero.' To his surprise, the NFL executives in DC responded, The Gobblers.'"

Then, to update the story about the press and media coverage that happened in the 1934 state championship game between Amarillo and Corpus Christi that is in the chapter on the Sandies, in that visit with coach Reeve, he brought out the fact that Gobbler football games are not only carried over the regular air waves, but also are carried on a website, KBAR FM out of Victoria. Coach Reeve told his team about the impact Gobbler football has around the world. According to the website stats, there were listeners in over 50 countries in the past season. Hits are the number that measure how many people listen to Cuero broadcasts around the world. The number was in the thousands last season.

In downtown Cuero in the Chamber of Commerce Building, formerly the U.S. Post Office, a museum dedicated to telling the story of Gobbler football is housed in two of the rooms. The museum is a labor of love created by a former Gobbler player Mike Weber from the class of 1952, and by Liz Heiser of Victoria. It is a work in progress as they have created the history in sections. The first section covers the 1911-1940 era. The second era runs from 1941-1972. The third section covers the Glory Years, 1973 to 1975. Weber stated that "The beginning of integration was the turning point in building Cuero's football fortunes. The good black athletes made us contenders." There is one wall that is dedicated to Daule High School football from 1942 to 1964. Daule was the black school that turned out some outstanding teams as illustrated in the boards on the wall. The boards hold pictures of the teams, some individual players and coaches, and display news clippings of individual games on all of these sections. There are panels featuring the Gobbler bands, cheerleaders and lists of players who went on to play in college and professionally.

During the Glory Years of 1972 to 1975, Cuero won 54 games while losing twice. Coach William "Buster" Gilbreth coached the Gobblers to the 1973 and 1974 AAA state championships. They were undefeated both years with 15-0 records each time. That streak continued through the 1975 season as the Gobblers ran up 44 straight wins, the fifth longest consecutive win streak in Texas high school football. Winning their first 14 games of the 75 season, Cuero tried for a three-peat, but Ennis stopped the streak as the Lions won the State Championship over Cuero 13-10.

There is a display case that holds a pair of shoes that played a role in the streak. The shoes are the green and white saddle oxfords that were worn by Debbie Gilbreth as a Gobbler cheerleader for all 45 games in those three years. She is the daughter of Coach Gilbreth. She was superstitious enough that she decided to wear the shoes all during the win streak. She didn't want her going to a new pair of shoes to play a role in the end of the streak. So despite the fact that one of the shoes had a big hole in the sole, she kept wearing them through all 45 games. The shoes are displayed in the case so that the hole in the one shoe prominently sticks out for viewing.

Her dad spent 28 years coaching high school football teams, beginning at Poteet in 1952 and ending at Fort Bend Clements in 1990 when he retired. His record for that span was 206-92-12. Clearly his greatest success came at Cuero. He began there in 1969 and moved after 1979. He coached the Gobblers to 107 wins against 22 losses and three ties in 11 years. There are a number of games and players from his time in Cuero that especially stand out to him. That is in addition to the experience for him and his family of being embraced and adored by one of the most football-crazy towns in Texas. In an interview in June, 2014, Gilbreth touched on all these points from his home in San Antonio.

He began with a summary of what his years as the Gobbler coach produced and how it impacted him and his family. "We had an incredible run in Cuero. During my tenure there we had four State Championship game appearances; 1970, '73, '74 & '75. We won the State Championship in '73 & '74. In 1970, we won our place to compete for the Zone (District) game by a coin toss due to a three-way tie. We were labeled the "Cinderella" team because we weren't the team anyone expected to win, but kept winning going all the way to the State game and played against Brownwood, losing 14-0. During the '73-75' seasons we had a 44-game winning streak, shutting out 26 opponents. The streak ended at the State game in '75. We made the playoffs nine of the 11 seasons while I was there, and this was at a time when only one team made it into the playoffs per zone/district. Cuero is also so special because the whole town, including school board, student body, parents, grandparents, etc. all came together in full support of the program. You could feel the backing of everyone and we were all "one" as a community. There was no black, white, rich or poor. We were all Gobblers. Especially during the winning streak years, there was an excitement that cannot be put into words. You just had to live it."

There were certain games that stood out for Gilbreth. He said, "The most exciting game was the 1973 Quarter-Final game against Gregory Portland. They were ranked #1 and we were #2 in the Harris ratings. They had a defense that had given up very few points and an offense that scored as much as they could on their opponents. Cuero played a perfectly executed game against them, shutting them down completely, winning 20-0." He went on to tell about the biggest district game that Cuero had during his years there. It was actually two games involving Uvalde in 1972 and 1973. He stated, "The biggest district games (called Zone then) were the Cuero vs. Uvalde match-ups. It started in 1972, and we were undefeated that season and were picked to make it to State. Uvalde beat us 14-7 and went on to win State that season. Our players didn't forget that loss and in 1973 we met Uvalde again for the "Zone Championship" game and beat them 20-0 and we went on to win the State Championship."

I asked Buster what was the biggest playoff game he coached there. He replied, "If you are asking what was the most "exciting" playoff game, it would be the Cuero vs. Brazosport game at Tully Stadium in 1974. Brazosport scored first to take the lead 6-0. Cuero scored right before the half to make it 7-6. No one scored in the third quarter, but in the fourth quarter with less than four minutes of play, Brazosport went ahead 13-7. On the kickoff to us after they scored, we returned the ball 65 yards to score and win this Bi-District game 14-13. But if you are asking me the "Biggest, most significant win", it would be the 1973 State Championship win against Mt. Pleasant 20-7 and the 1974 State Championship win against Gainesville 19-7. There is no win that can compare to a State Championship win."

Gilbreth recalled some of the Gobbler players that stood out to him on offense during his tenure there, "Arthur Whittington from the 1973 team stands out. He had speed, durability and commitment. He played both ways (RB & Safety), an incredible athlete. He went on to play for SMU and then the Oakland Raiders (was on Super Bowl XV team). Also on the 1974 team were David Hill (TB/CB) and Marion Harper (FB/LB), both with incredible speed and dedication and both going on to play for SMU." Asked about defensive players, Gilbreth responded, "Henry Sheppard on the 1970 team (DE & T). He was a dominating player and a leader who went on to play for SMU and the Cleveland Browns. Also on that 1970 team was Lloyd Wesley (LB), who was the best LB I've ever coached. From the '73 & '74 team was Calvin Blackwell (DE & T) who was also a dominating player, giving it his all every play. He went on to play for SMU.

The running game was definitely a part of the Cuero offense during those years. Gilbreth had five different players go over 1000 yards rushing for the season during that time, a span of six years. He had mentioned Whittington first as one of his standout players. In 1973, their first year of the streak, Whittington rushed for 1528 yards. The second 1000 yard rusher in 1973 was Nathaniel Johnson with 1359 yards. In 1974, two more Gobblers stepped up to the line and crossed over it freely picking up big yardage again. Hill, another one of the players singled out by Gilbreth as one of the best Gobblers ever led another duo of Gobbler rushers crashing the 1000 yard barrier with 1485 yards. Gary Pickens was behind him with 1100 yards. Wesley is credited with gaining 1158 yards.

In the period of 1983 through 1985, the Gobblers were led by a quarterback who was the leading passer in Class 3A in 1984 with 2526 yards and 31 touchdown passes. Brad Goebel helped Cuero win 80% of their games while he played. The Gobblers won 32 games and lost eight during this three year span, topped off by reaching the 1985 3A State Championship game. Below is his interview with me in early August, 2014 from his home at Horseshoe Bay where he and his wife, Kristi, have a real estate company. I began asking him how far Cuero had advanced in the playoffs each year he played for them. It was Bi-District in 1983 losing to Median Valley 23-21. In his junior year, the Gobblers beat Aransas Pass in Bi-District 24-14; Hebronville in Area 35-8 and lost in Regional to Columbia 35-7. In 1985, they won the first five playoff games including a thriller over Van Vleck in the Semi-Finals 38-36 on a field goal with five seconds left on the clock. There are additional comments about that game after Goebel's interview. The Gobblers won the first four games before that in the following order: Bi-District over Sinton 35-7, Area over Sharyland 20-10, Regional over Medina Valley 14-7 and Quarter- Finals over San Antonio Cole 49-14. Daingerfield beat them for the 3A title 47-22.

He commented about playing football in Cuero and other smaller towns like it, "Football in a small town unites the community and gives pride to the town. Cuero had a history of successful football teams when I was growing up and we felt it was our responsibility to continue the tradition. It was expected and we felt that and embraced it." He continued talking about his coach on the Gobblers, "My head coach in Cuero was Larry Pullin. He was and still is a very close dear friend. We still talk each week and play a lot of golf together. Coach Pullin was unique because he figured out how to motivate each player. He instilled discipline from the start but allowed guys to be individuals as long as they didn't cross the line. I still remember the fact that he would go pick up some players from their houses to get them to practice because they didn't have any transportation. Some didn't have very good families, but Coach Pullin was a father figure to them and all of us."

Goebel recalled some significant games during his years there beginning with some district games, "We played Beeville High my junior year and that was my first varsity start having played WR before then. I threw an interception on the one yard line and it was returned for a TD by Beeville 99 yards. We got beat in that game, but Coach Pullin came up to me after the game and had a big smile on his face and told me that he had found his QB of the future and that I was going to be a great player. The following year we played Beeville again and this time beat them pretty bad. I remember one play in particular when I had scrambled toward the Cuero sidelines and threw the ball away as I was getting tackled. I was flagged for intentional grounding and when I got up, Coach Pullin was in my face screaming at me. I was embarrassed and disappointed in my actions, but the very next play, Coach called another pass play and I went through my progression and ultimately found my fourth receiver streaking down the sideline as I hit him in stride for a 60 yard TD pass. When I came to the sidelines, Coach Pullin just smiled and said great job and praised me like nothing ever happened on the prior play."

The Van Vleck game in the Semi-Finals in 1985 was his next memory, "We had a showdown with Van Vleck in the State Semi- Final game my senior year at Memorial Stadium in Austin. Van Vleck had been rated #1 all year and we upset them thanks to a last second field goal by Clay Pullin, Coach Pullin's son. Prior to that kick, we drove down the length of the field with short passes and versions of the "two-minute drill". It was magical to see how our whole team came together and made plays to get us in position to win that game."

Brad closed with how he continues to promote to current Gobbler players the specialness of playing for Cuero. With his great play at Baylor where he earned a scholarship to play football, followed by his five-year stay in the NFL, Goebel certainly makes an impact when he gets to go back and speak to the current Gobbler team members. He closed with comments about his trips back to Cuero, "I have gone back to Cuero several times to watch games and root the team on. My parents still live in Cuero and I have had several cousins and relatives to play for the Gobblers. Last year they inducted me into the Cuero High School Hall of Fame which was a special honor for me. I was asked to talk to the football team before the game and I did, telling them how special it was to play for the Gobblers and I expected them to continue the traditions."

That Semi-Final win over Van Vleck in 1985 at Memorial Stadium in Austin was mentioned to me by sports writers from other towns in South Texas as being perhaps the most exciting playoff game the Gobblers ever played. The Leopards' coach, Bill McGonale, was quoted as thinking the game would be a defensive struggle. Most of the pigskin prognosticators around the state seconded his opinion with predictions of a low scoring game. The Leopards were 13-0 with playoff wins 42-20 over Cleveland in Bi-District, 26-12 over #1 Navasota in Regional and 10-3 over Port Arthur Austin in the Area round.

The game would turn out to be a shootout. The Gobblers were loaded with key skill position players who could put points on the board with ease. As mentioned above, Goebel was the quarterback and Clay Pullin, who would be the game hero, was a wingback. Danny Stewart and freshman Robert Strait were the running backs. Carlos Taylor was the wide receiver and Brian Parks the tight end. Cuero ran up a 28-14 halftime lead and added to it halfway through the third quarter as the Gobblers ended a 15-play, 56-yard drive with Strait going over from the two yard line for a 35-14 Gobbler lead.

Van Vleck had its own top quarterback, Robert Blackmon, who rallied the Leopards with touchdown passes of five and 37 yards in the rest of the third period to make the score 35-29 Cuero as the period ended. Van Vleck got to the Cuero nine-yard line early in the fourth period, but came away with no points. Strait appeared to give the Gobblers some extra insurance as he raced 88 yards for an apparent touchdown. It was called back for Cuero being in illegal motion as the play began. Two turnovers by Cuero in the fourth put the Gobblers under additional pressure. Stewart lost a fumble at the Cuero 35. Then Van Vleck intercepted a Goebel pass on the Cuero 26 yard line. The Leopards scored on a 26 yard touchdown pass by Blackmon with 4:03 left in the game. The score gave the Leopards their first lead in the game at 36-35.

Cuero got the ball on its 48 yard line to begin its final drive. A 15-yard penalty on the Leopards moved the ball to their 47 yard line. In seven plays, the big one being a 12 yard pass completion from Goebel to Taylor, Cuero moved to the 11 yard line. The Gobblers missed on a first down pass on the first play. Strait carried for two yards. Both schools called timeouts before Pullin lined up to kick his game winning 26-yard field goal with five seconds on the clock. That put Cuero in the State Championship game in Waco at Baylor Stadium the next week. It was an exciting win for the Gobblers. For Goebel, playing at Baylor Stadium in his final high school game was memorable because it was where he would star for the Baylor Bears the next four years.

The Gobblers are not only fortunate enough to have multiple generations from one family playing for the team, they are also fortunate enough to have multiple generation coaches. From 2003 to 2009, Mark Reeve coached Cuero. He ran up a stellar record of 83-11-0 in that seven year span. One of his assistants was his son, Travis Reeve. Now for the past two seasons, Travis has been the head coach. He stands 13-10-0 for the 2012 and 2013 seasons. He was 5-6 his first year and 8-4 last season. He had some good comments about coaching there, some of the good games he has coached, some of the key players that have been under his guidance and the outlook for 2014.

He began, "Cuero has such a long tradition of success that it is hard not to be excited about what you do each and every day. Kids growing up in Cuero want to be part of that tradition and they really work hard to live up to the standard that others have set before them. Also, the community support for what we do is second to none. We have the greatest fans in the state of Texas and they are what makes the Friday night experience special in Cuero."

He discussed some of the games he had been involved in either as an assistant coach or as a head coach for the Gobblers, "The most exciting game was probably our win over Palestine 27-17 in the 2004 State Semi-Finals. I was an assistant at that time to Mark Reeve and that win punched our ticket to the State Championship game. As a head coach, a come-from-behind win versus Wharton (20-19) in our season opener of my first year (2012) and a 21-13 win over LaGrange, who was previously undefeated, in the last game of the season to make the playoffs were two of the more exciting games we have had. We had to win the LaGrange game to make the playoffs. Our kids played great that night, allowing us to get in the playoffs. As an assistant, I remember in 2009 we played Yoakum, who had traditionally been a very big rivalry game, during district play and we had to come from behind to beat them 26-23 in the last minute of the game. They had a good team and played well that night and we were fortunate to find a way to win. Our biggest playoff game was the 2004 3A-Division II State Championship versus Abilene Wylie. Unfortunately, we lost on a last second field goal 17-14, but it was a great year and a great group of young men."

Reeve recalled some of the top players he had coached, "We have been fortunate to have had a lot of great players in Cuero. We have had some outstanding tailbacks in Latrell Cooper, Fabian Olguin, Larvell Roy, Quincy Whittington, Trent Jackson and currently D'Anthony Hopkins. At quarterback, Matt Schumacher and Kyle Noack were outstanding leaders and competitors and Tyler Arndt, who started for us for three years leading us to three Semi-Final appearances, was probably the most talented QB we had during those years. At wide receiver, Robert Armstrong and Tre Gray were two of the most explosive players I have ever coached."

He moved on to defensive standouts for the Gobblers, beginning, "In the secondary Jeremy Ross was an exceptional safety and Martell Williams was a really good corner. J.T. Rudd, Joey Adams, Kaeron Johnson and Stephon Hargrove were dominant defensive lineman."

About the upcoming 2014 season, Reeve commented, "We are looking forward to a great 2014. We have lots of kids coming back from a good year in 2013 and have some talented young players moving up to the varsity."

THE HIGHLAND PARK SCOTS

FIRST YEAR THEY PLAYED: 1923
ALL-TIME RECORD THROUGH 2013: 767-250-27
PERCENTAGE: 74.76%
STATE CHAMPIONSHIP GAMES WON: 1945, 1957, 2005
STATE CHAMPIONSHIP GAMES LOST: 1944, 1947, 2007

I thought I would set the matter straight and save any debate upfront. There is no rival to the record compiled by the Scots since they first played in 1923. In total wins, they have 24 more than the second place Sandies. One comparison of that number that came to mind is the gap in total wins between them and the Odessa Permian Panthers. I pick on Permian because there are so many people who just know that the West Texas school is the all-time leader, thanks to all the publicity generated by the Friday Night Lights book, movie and TV series. Here's a stat to show how far a difference exists between those two schools' victories. Suppose the UIL changed the rules and all schools could only play 10 games a year, no playoffs beyond. Then suppose Permian went on a streak and won all their games each year while Highland Park started its own streak of losing all its games each year. It would take Permian 27 years until 2041 to catch up with the Scots. Permian has 492 wins through 2013 to the Scots' 767 wins.

Still need some convincing about the Scots? In total losses among the 12 schools featured in this book, the Scots have 250 losses on their record. The next school in fewest total losses is the Hondo Owls with 318, 68 more than the Scots. In terms of winning percentage, the Scots as shown above have a 74.76% record to date. Amarillo has the next highest percentage at 68.42%, some 6.34% below the Scots. Still not convinced about the Scots? Notice they played their first game in 1923, some 10 years later than the next youngest team in the group. So to summarize, Highland Park has 24 more wins, 68 fewer losses, nearly a 10% higher winning percentage than any other of our elite teams. And they have done it all in at least 10 years less than our other teams. Enough said, here's the rest of their story to date.

Perhaps, divine intervention could have also played a role in the success of the Scots, at least in the case of their first State Championship in 1945, a co-championship after a 7-7 tie with Waco High. The famed sportswriter of the Southwest, Harold V. Ratliff, told this story in his 1953 collection of sports stories for all occasions, *It was like this.* "Highland Park and Waco were playing in Dallas for the Texas high school football championship. The score was tied at 7-7. There were only minutes to go and James (Froggie) Williams of Waco was preparing to attempt a field goal from the Highland Park 20-yard line. Herman Morgan, the assistant Highland Park coach, moved down to the end of the bench where he could pray a little without the others hearing. 'Oh God,' said Morgan lowly, 'don't let Williams kick that field goal.' Then he felt an arm around his shoulders and Eck Curtis, the head coach, breathed into Morgan's ear: 'Yes Lord, be with us now.' Williams missed the field goal and the teams tied for the championship."

Highland Park came into existence in 1922, initially picking the Coyote to be its mascot and the school colors to be orange and black. Highland Park formed its first team the next year with Floyd Betts as the coach. Gradually, the mascot evolved into the Highlanders. The school colors were changed to blue and gold. Sometime in the early 1940s, the fans began calling them the Scots. They named a Scottish Terrier as the mascot in 1947. Soon the team name evolved into the Scots. Of course, plaid is associated with the Scots. So today, a drive around Highland Park provides plenty of sightings of the blue and gold colored plaid signs placed in virtually every yard in the neighborhood stating that the family there is "Proud of the Plaid." On November 18, 1977, they added the Fighting Scot as a symbol.

The Scots have their own stadium on campus, Highlander Stadium. A beautiful red brick structure, it offers spectators a closer view of the field since there is no track around the field. It took nearly two years to build the stadium. During the first year of construction, 1979, the Scots played their home games at the SMU field, Ownby Stadium. For the first six games of the 1980 stadium, Highland Park took a page from the Plano Wildcats and played at Texas Stadium. They played their first game in Highlander on October 24, 1980.

When you think of the Scots, one of the first players for them that comes to mind is Doak Walker. He was in the same backfield with Bobby Layne during his playing time there. What a dynamite combination of talent. After he finished playing for the Scots in 1944, he went to SMU where he proceeded to become a three time All-American and the Heisman Trophy winner. He was so popular and beloved that in 1949 the old Dallas Times-Herald published a series of articles about his entire football career beginning as a three year old. Walker wrote many of the articles himself including about his time at Highland Park. I was fortunate that my grandmother, Emma Riddle, had taught Walker in the third grade at Armstrong Elementary in the Highland Park school system. She befriended him and his family. So when he began to write his memoirs, she was clipping the articles from the Times Herald to create a scrap book for me on my ninth birthday and added other articles and pictures of Doak to make it a unique gift for me. It's like getting to interview him personally to present what he wrote for the Times Herald 65 years ago about his career with the Scots.

He began, "In September of 1941, I entered Highland Park High School. What a great experience that was! I was going to get to play now with the boys who were the best. Clifton Wilhite and Orr were coaches. Wilhite was a former SMU basketball player and he was really a slick. Junior Ethridge and I played on the "B" team. I was right half and Junior was fullback. We played that old Notre Dame box... a balanced line with single wing in the right. Junior and I were carrying the ball on reverses from this formation. We thought we could really scat. I remember that both of us had brown helmets."

He spoke of getting hurt, "My first real injury from football occurred this season. I split one of the fingers on my left hand while making a tackle in a scrimmage with the South Dallas "B" team. It took about three weeks for me to get over the injury, but even before I could play again, I was on the practice field running to keep my legs in shape."

Then he talked of learning backfield skills, "This year I improved on some very important points for a backfield man. I learned how to use my blockers in running, how to get up a block and how to put myself in motion with the least amount of time or effort. Getting into motion in a hurry is one of the greatest assets I think a ball carrier can have. I learned to control my balance and start fast with the first step.

I learned too, that when you're running down field and see a defender that a blocker is going to try for, you should try to get the blocker between yourself and the defender. If necessary, slow down a little, change pace. The ability to do a thing like this comes from practice, practice, practice, plus a certain amount of native ability."

Walker continued,"All of that goes along with learning how to set up a block. Another example would be like this: I am running down the field and have a blocker in front of me who is going to try for a defender. I am going to feint in such a way that the defender will come in from an angle that will help the blocker get him handily. I became a little more proficient too, on punt returns. I learned that my blockers were supposed to be at certain places and that I had to think fast enough to set up my run accordingly."

"Anyway Jack Jones, George Martin and I were sent to the "A" squad about four weeks before the season was over. I'll never forget that first day if I live to be a hundred. We were strictly live bait. They put me on the defensive right end and told me to rush the passer. Hey, I guessed they put me there to see if I could take it. They really roughed me up, and, believe me, I was sore, sore, sore. When they started scrimmaging, they put me at defensive halfback and Sharp, Hall and Redman nearly tore me up. I was sore every night just as if I had been in a whale of a game. I'll say one thing though. That Redman, his first name is David, made a tackler out of me. That's a boy who could really go. He was one of those fellows who could be going full blast after his first step."

About learning to tackle, Walker commented,"I had to get him or else. He'd come off on a reverse and cut through a hole and for a week he ran over me. Finally I got so I could catch him. A little later I could drive into him and hold him. Then I got a big thrill when I was 'ble not only to catch and hold him but to drive him back. Incidentally when I moved up to the 'A" squad, the coaches were Hume and Hightower."

About his second year on the Scots, Walker said, "The season of 1942, Ted Munnell and Redman were co-captains. Humes had left to take a job on the SMU coaching staff and Hightower was head coach at Highland Park. Albert Dudley was assistant coach. About midseason, Coach Rusty Russell came over from Masonic Home in Fort Worth after we had beaten his team 28-9. They had us 9-7 at the half. But we came through. That was Hightower's last ball game before he left to go into the Navy."

Football camp was part of his time at Highland Park, "But I'm getting a little ahead of my story. This was my first year at football camp. We were housed at Camp Kiwanis near Duncanville and all we had to do for 10 wonderful days was eat, sleep, drink and digest football. Newcomers at the camp were stooges for the old hands and I was Layne's stooge. He would make me raid the icebox at night for fruit and milk and stuff like that. Football camp was a lot of fun as well as a lot of work. I remember one joker who asked the coach if he would have time to go hunting while we were in camp. The coach told him, 'Sure you'll have plenty of time to go hunting, but you won't feel like it.'

At night after lights out there was usually a little scuffling and horseplay before things settled down. I remember one night Coach Hightower caught one of the boys and sent him out in front of the camp and told him to start running laps around a clearing. The coach went on to sleep and forgot all about the poor guy and he spent half the night jogging outside.

Another time the coach told someone to get the tackling dummy from the practice field which was almost two miles from camp, and after the fellow had lugged the dummy all the way in, the coach made him turn around and take it back."

He added, "I weighed about 135 pounds when camp was over. That was one time when I was really in shape. That Hightower had a mania for physical training. It was at this camp that I acquired the name of Silent Pete. I never have been much of a talker and when the coach would ask me my assignment on a play, I would just point in the direction I was supposed to go or wave toward the man I was supposed to get. Pretty soon, all the fellows began calling me Silent Pete and telling me not to make so much racket."

Walker said, "I was the fifth man in the backfield that year. Whoever came out, I went in and I gained all kinds of experience. I will remember the first day that Coach Russell showed up. We really thought he was going to be a nail-biter. All year we had been hitting dummies in tackling practice and the first day Russell told us to line up against each other for this practice. We asked him if we weren't going to use the dummies and he replied, 'Boys, when they start using dummies in football games, that's the day we will start using them in practice.' From then on, you might say we used each other."

About Rusty Russell, Walker commented, "Coach Russell didn't try to change our formations or anything that year because, as I said, it was midseason when he took over and I guess he figured the best thing to do was let us go ahead and play the season out as we were. This was the year that we got beat 13-7 by Sunset High School in the Quarter-Finals of the state race. We had a pretty good team. The boys seemed to work well together. "

Initially Walker missed as a kicker as he relates, "To go back a little, it was this season, too, they began to use me to kick extra points. I'll never forget the first three I tried. I think we were playing Dallas Tech in an early season game. We scored early in the first quarter and Coach Hightower sent me in to kick the point. I missed and as I trotted off the field, I felt awful. A little later we scored again and Hightower sent me in to try for the point once more. Again I missed and I figured that my football career was drawing rapidly to a close. I just knew that the coach was going to rake me over the coals. He didn't say a word, however. "

"A little later, we scored again and Hightower nodded to me and said, 'Go in and get that point Doak.' This time my kick sailed between the uprights and I came off the field feeling like a different guy. Hightower patted me on the back and encouraged me and I really felt like I had contributed something. I don't know why Hightower decided to try me on the extra points. I guess it was just a hunch on his part. Anyway I went on to kick a good many that year and in the process, I acquired another nickname. It was the Sulphuric Sophomore with The Educated Toe. I didn't get to handle the ball too much that year because they had some mighty good boys in the backfield, but I was willing to wait for my chance. That year I had jersey number 94, I remember."

Walker described some of his other sports participation and his time back in the summer camp in a few sentences before resuming his recollections of the Russell era at Highland Park. Then he continued, "The year 1943 was Rusty Russell's first full season at Highland Park as head coach. His assistant was Herman Morgan. Dudley, who had been Hightower's assistant, had gone in the Navy by now, too. This year, Russell put his own ideas into practice and we knew right quick that we had both a taskmaster and a smart coach. We used to say that the games were a cinch to play after the long rough practice Russell put us through all week and we weren't kidding either. What a guy!"

Coach Russell changed routines up as Walker recalled, "I remember it was our custom after a Friday night game in the early part of the season to show up at school on Saturday morning, put on some shorts and shoes and toss the ball around for an hour just to limber up. Then we'd go home. But our new coach changed all of that in a hurry. The first Saturday morning after a game, we started out to the practice field in our shorts and Coach Russell said, 'What goes on here fellows? Where are your pads?' We thought he was joking so we made some wisecrack and he said, 'Go get those pads on. Let's go. Let's go!' We knew by now that he wasn't fooling for sure and we went back to the dressing room and suited out and do you know that he put us through a light scrimmage that morning. Yes sir! We were beginning to understand now why those Masonic Home teams coached by Russell had been so tough. Yeah, the guys who weren't pretty tough couldn't take the workouts!"

He continued, "On another occasion I remember that Layne and I were alternating at half on an off tackle play. Coach Russell didn't think that we had the timing down right and we ran that one play over and over all morning long. And I'll guarantee you we could have run that play in our sleep by the time that practice session was over. This season Russell had us using some double wing and some spread formations."

Walker told of being elected co-captain, "Layne and I were elected co-captains and believe me, this is a job that carries plenty of responsibility along with it. The honor is swell and it means a lot, but if you're a captain, you got to be in there hustling just a little harder than the other guys all the time because you've got to set an example for the other fellows both on and off the field. In a game, too, you've got to provide leadership and keep the team hustling.

The boys have put their faith in you and you've got to do the best you can for them."

He went on about the team in the playoffs, "We went to the state Semi-Finals that year and got beat 21-20 by San Angelo on their home field. They had a fine ball club, but we should have beat them. In fact, we were beating them up until the last quarter. At that point we were ahead 20-7 and then something happened. I really believe that the altitude had something to do with it because up until then, we had been playing good ball. Anyway we got beat."

About teaming up with Layne, Doak gushed, "I had a lot of fun going out and catching Layne's passes. That boy can really throw that ball. We were a pretty good combination if I do say so myself. I was playing safety on defense and I remember that in the offense, we used a lot of reverses and flicker plays that were just right for Layne's style. Bobby had a lot of natural ability when it comes to sports. A little practice and he can do most anything. The first summer he took up golf, he was shooting in the low 80s in no time. If he wanted to be a pro golfer, I believe he could. He could do the same thing in basketball."

Back to the play on the field, he said, "I remember one game in particular this season in which Junior Eldridge really took a beating. I thought they were going to kill him in the Wichita Falls game because they hit him so hard on punt returns. Wichita Falls punted and the big ends went down and smashed into Junior. An off sides was called on the play so it had to be run over. They punted again and Junior started out with the ball and the big ends nearly tore him in half. Another off sides was called and the play was run over for the third time. Again Junior got the ball and again those big ends smashed into him. I wondered if he would be able to get up, but he made it. Junior is little, but he is really rugged. He had to be to take punishment like that. I was mighty proud this year when I got Honorable Mention for the All-State squad. I also received the school award as the most valuable blocking back."

Walker talked about the 1944 season, "This was Layne's last year and he went on to the University of Texas on a baseball scholarship. He was a pitcher and an excellent one too. I'm not sure that he ever planned to go out for football when he went to Texas. My jersey number for 1943 and 1944 was number 84. The season of 1944, I was elected co-captain at Highland Park High School along with Bob Tenison who was a good tackle. With Russell and Morgan coaching again, we had about the same squad as the one in 1943 and this made it a pretty easy squad to work. I could tell that I had improved a good deal when the season opened. In fact, it was the first season I can remember where any great improvement was apparent to me. I had more speed and I could turn it on when I needed it. I knew that I had that extra burst because I could feel the surge of speed whenever I really tried for it. That, by the way, was what I lacked the year before and was the reason I was bumped out of bounds or tackled so often on the one, two or three-yard line."

"During the season of 1943 it just seemed that I couldn't get over that goal line like I should. I know now that what I lacked was that little extra spurt. Well, I had it now and it was paying off. I think a lot of us during 1943 and 1944 had a hard time keeping our minds on football. The country was at war and many of the boys on the squad wanted to get on in there. I know that we talked a lot about what branch of the service we wanted to get in, etc. Anyway we had a pretty good season and went clear to the State Finals, where we were bumped by a rough, tough team from Port Arthur. The game was played at Austin and we ended up on the short end of the 19-7 score. We made only one touchdown when I passed to Clark. I kicked the extra point. "

He closed his comments, "This you might say was my swan song to my high school career. I sure hated to see it end and because, it meant that I wouldn't see much of swell fellows again. Anyway, I got some extra kicks out of that season because I made the All-State team, the All-Southern team and was voted the most valuable player on the club. I was also invited to play in the North-South high school football game and in the Oil Bowl at Wichita Falls, but I had to turn down these invitations because I was entering the service."

The year 1957 was supposed to be Amarillo High's year to be the 4A state football champion. If that scenario didn't happen, then it was supposed that defending state champion Abilene would go on to its fifty-first straight victory and fourth State Championship in a row; instead Highland Park won its second State Championship. The Scots were coached by Thurman 'Tugboat' Jones. He guided them to an 11-1-1 record as they scored 424 points and allowed only 76 points. In Bi-District, the Scots beat Crozier Tech for the second year in a row at that level, this time by a 26-7 margin. Next, they avenged a prior year Quarter-Final loss to Wichita Falls by a 19-7 edge. Instead of Amarillo being their Semi-Final opponent as had been predicted, they caught an Abilene Eagle team fresh off a 33-14 win over the Sandies, their forty-ninth straight victory. The two teams tied 20-20, but Highland Park advanced on a 5-3 edge in penetrations inside their opponents' 20 yard line. They easily handled Port Arthur 21-9 for the 4A State Championship.

Among the most beloved and highly respected players who led the Scots at the key quarterback position is Lance McIlhenny. He characterized the Scots as being 'a bunch of average white guys trying to overachieve.' His coach was Frank Bevers who he said, 'had a great offensive mind featuring the Houston veer.' He handled the Veer pretty well as the Scots had a 39-7 record during the four years he was on the team, though as a freshman, he was just brought up for the playoffs. As a sophomore, he was named the Newcomer of the Year in the district. That was 1977 when they met Plano in the Quarter-Finals and gave up a 28-0 lead losing to the Wildcats 29-28. McIlhenny had scored two touchdowns by rushing and passed for two more to get the Scots that lead. The team gradually saw the lead reduced as Plano rallied against the Scot defense for two scores. McIlhenny commented, "I pitched the ball while running the veer and their cornerback took it for six the other way." That accounted for the only Plano defensive score. The Scots defense in the last minute gave up a 61-yard touchdown pass and the Wildcats gambled and went for two points to get the win.

He went on a scholarship to play quarterback for SMU and led it to a 34-5-1 record, tops in the Southwest Conference. Today he is a commercial real estate broker. About his time playing for Highland Park, McIlhenny says, "The tradition of Highland Park football feeds on itself. Some of the greatest times of my life."

In my chapter on Recognition, I had mentioned David Richards who in 1983 was a Parade All-American from Highland Park and just happened to be chosen the national highs school player of the year by Parade Magazine. He was an offensive lineman for the Scots before going on to play for SMU and UCLA. Like father, like son, I met his son, Tony Richards on July 21, 2014, in San Antonio. Tony had been chosen as an offensive linemen from Highland Park to play in the Texas High School Coaching School All-Star football game. A highly congenial young man, he fits the mold of what being a Scot is all about. He gave me the following comments about his time at Highland Park. "I was a two year varsity player for Highland Park. In my junior year, we lost in the first round of the playoffs to Frisco High School and in my senior year, we lost in the Semi-Finals to Denton Guyer."

He expanded on his time on the Scots, "I didn't play hardly at all my junior year, but my senior year, I made undisputed All-District, Honorable Mention All-State, the TXA 21 All North Texas and played in the All-Star football game. I have a scholarship to play at SMU. The main thing that made playing at Highland Park special was the tradition. We had a lots of guys on our team who had fathers, uncles and grandfathers that played here. Then there was the program and the pep rallies and everything like that that hasn't really changed that much since the program began. It is much the same as it was when my dad played here."

Richards spoke about his coach, "Playing for coach Randy Allen was a lot of fun. In my time there, he made a lot of gutsy calls that worked in our favor, and along with the rest of the coaching staff, always were able to put us in a position to be successful and a lot of the time, we were."

Speaking about some of the key games for Highland Park while he played, he commented," My junior year we played Mesquite Poteet and it came down to the last few seconds. We were down by seven. We got a long pass down the sideline and scored with like six or seven seconds left. We went for two and the win and got it (20-19). I didn't play at all, but it was still a really great experience. The next year we played them at home and they were predicted to win and end our 83 game home winning streak. We came out and won by a big margin (41-26). I didn't really have any key blocks, but generally our offensive line played really well. Our pass protection was the key to our win."

Tony continued with his recall of key playoff games, "The first round of the playoffs my senior year was really important seeing as we had lost that game the year before. We were playing the Colony. We were predicted to lose (like all of our playoff games). Our defense played really well to stop their powerhouse running game. The play that put it away was a stretch play down the left side. I hooked the defensive end who was lined up several yards outside of me. That allowed the running back to turn the corner for a 30 something yard run for a touchdown." Highland Park won 38-17.

He concluded his remarks with further comments about the Scot tradition, "Since we were young, we were all told how special it was to play for the Scots and how the tradition of winning and playing with sportsmanship and respect for the game was so important. We all did our part to make sure that the younger kids coming in understood and hold it to the standards we were held to by the guys older than us. I don't think that I did anything on an individual level to promote the Highland Park tradition, but as a team I feel we did a very good job. And that's what I think is the key component of all this is that everything we did, we did it as a team, not individuals. That's what I think makes Highland Park so successful and so special."

Tony and all the other Scots are reminded every time they go into the team meeting room at the top of Highlander Stadium of just how special the Scot tradition in football is. On one wall is a sign on a gold background that gets updated each year. It shows exactly what Highland Park has accomplished on the football field since it began playing in 1923. I was there on August 13, 2014, to see Coach Allen and took the time to write down what is on the gold sign. It shows an all-time winning percentage of 74.5%. It lists a consistency rating of 494, a number that depicts how many more wins the Scots have than their total losses. There have been 34 10-win seasons. In the past 12 years, the Scots have had 47 consecutive regular season wins from 2005 to2008. There have been 79 consecutive home wins. In district, their 12 year record is 73-2. There was a 26 game winning streak from 2005 into 2006. The Scots have been in twelve district playoff games, ten Bi-District games, eight Area games, four Quarter-Final games, two Semi-Final games, two Final games and one State Championship. Their record in Class 4A games from 2000 through 2010 is 118-14. Their players are reminded that the Scots have the most district championships in Texas with forty-seven titles, the most playoff appearances getting into games in fifty-five seasons. They have been in thirty-six Area games, twenty-eight Quarter-Final games, sixteen Semi-Final games and the six State Championship games listed at the beginning of this chapter. There is also a list of the Scots who have gone on to play in the NFL.

In the chapter, *Football, a family tradition*, one of the Highland Park families we profiled was the Jack Sides family. Jack D. Sides III played for the Scots varsity in 1985, 1986 and 1987. He did an interview for us about his playing time on the team. He played fullback as a sophomore and outside linebacker his junior and senior years. The Scots failed to get out of district in his sophomore and senior years, but made it to the third round in his junior year in 1986. He recounts his time on the Scots in the following interview.

"In 1986, I was a second team All-District linebacker, 1987 Honorable Mention All-District Defensive End (It was determined by district coaches at the time because of our new 3-4 defensive scheme that I would be considered a defensive end for purposes of voting in post season honors…still confused by that!); I received Highland Park's Fightin'est Scot Award after my senior season…very meaningful to me…this plaque hangs inside the stadium and lists the winners from every season… a great group of guys to be associated with. I was an invited walk-on at SMU in Forrest Gregg's first year as head coach after the SMU death penalty."

Sides says that, "tradition, community and success", makes playing at Highland Park such a special experience. Then he spoke about his coach, "My head coach was Randy Emery. He had been a long time, very successful defensive coordinator under Coach Frank Bevers. He had a short head coaching tenure at Highland Park…four years. I was with him for three of his four seasons. We had one successful season…my junior year (1986). Unfortunately my years were the transition years after the Frank Bevers era and weren't as successful as I would have liked. But, we learned a lot of tough life lessons, won some big games, got to play in Texas Stadium and the Cotton Bowl and experienced the magic of a HP football playoff run."

He continued about some of the big games he played in for the Scots, "I think the Mesquite game my junior year (1986). We beat them handily 49-10 and I had two interceptions in the game. This game was important because we locked up a playoff spot after missing the playoffs the prior season in Coach Emery's first season as a head coach." In playoff games, Sides responded, "Our game versus Dallas Carter in the Cotton Bowl in the second round of the playoffs my junior year is most memorable. This is the same Dallas Carter football program that was made famous by the movie *Friday Night Lights*. They were loaded with talent. Their biggest star was running back Darren Lewis who went on to star for Texas A & M in the Southwest Conference. It was a very tight game at the half. We pulled away in the second half and won impressively 31-11. I had an interception late in the game….a pass from future Texas Tech star Robert Hall intended for future Texas A & M star Darren Lewis. It was a special night….beating a very talented Dallas Carter team led by Darren Lewis in the 'House that Doak Built' in the playoffs."

Asked about his continuing support of the Highland Park program, Sides replied, "My son (Jack Sides) is a current player and I support him, his teammates and his coaches in all of their endeavors…. but this is their time. I always attend and support and observe and cheer loudly….I love it!!! But again, this is their time and they have their own magic and they fully understand where they are and what they are doing. Their team slogan in 2013 was 'The Tradition Continues' and their slogan for 2014 is 'A Texas Tradition'… that says it all."

There have been a number of successful high school football coaches at Highland Park since its inception-men like Redman Humes, Rusty Russell, Thurman "Tugboat" Jones and Frank Bevers. Jones and Bevers each coached the Scots at two different times indicating that they were well thought of by the Highland Park Board of Trustees. Still the current Scot coach, Randy Allen, is hands down, the best ever as Highland Park's head coach. He has a 174-21 record since 1999 for a winning percentage of 89.23%. The Scots won the Class 4A, Division I State Championship in 2005 lambasting Marshal 59-0 and played for the 2007 Class 4A, Division II State Championship getting edged by Lake Travis 36-34 in Waco. That winning percentage at Highland Park is moving his career percentage numbers up dramatically. In thirty-three years, he has a 326-80-6 record which by my eyeball estimate of those numbers has Allen winning 80% of his games. He began his career coaching at Ballinger in 1981-85. For the next five years, he was at Brownwood. He discusses his time coaching the Lions in the Brownwood chapter of *Friday's Winners*. From Brownwood, he moved to Abilene Cooper for the years 1991 through 1998. Then he came to Highland Park where he has coached fourteen years. He discusses his feelings about the school and the community, some of the key games for the Scots that he has coached, players who stood out to him and the upcoming 2014 season in the paragraphs below.

Allen began, "In some ways Highland Park is like a small town with an attitude. Highland Park welcomed my family like no other place. The applause and attention I got from the players was tremendous. My wife was given a welcome at the Dallas Country Club by some of her friends and all the football moms were given an invitation to come to meet her.

The team had ownership of the tradition. When I came, Highland Park was third in all time wins. Amarillo and Plano had more wins. Highland Park now has the most wins of any team in Texas high school history with 767 victories. There is great pride in being a Highland Park Scot that starts when the children are in elementary school. The elementary students dream of the day they will wear the blue and gold and represent Highland Park in high school. Many of our players have dads who played here. Each team we have coached has wanted to leave Highland Park football better than they found it.

Our players come from families who are successful so they have the attitude that they are going to be successful. They are very goal oriented and want to attend the best universities. Academics is very important to the students and they work very hard to keep their grades up.

Once a Scot, always a Scot. Our former players come back to the high school to lift weights and talk to the coaches. That is something I really enjoy.

The school motto is-Enter to Learn, Go forth to Serve. Our students represent our community well after they leave. There is a strong sense that since they have been blessed with material things, they have an obligation to give back to their school and community."

Coach Allen began discussing some of the games most meaningful to him. "Highland Park beat Mesquite Poteet last year at home after most of the sports writers of the Dallas Morning News had picked Poteet to win the game. It kept our home winning streak alive for the fifteenth year. In playoff games, we defeated Stephenville 41-38 in the State Semi-Finals in 2005 on our way to the State Championship."

He discussed the top Scots he's coached on offense and defense. "Matthew Stafford at quarterback. He was the best quarterback and the #1 draft pick in the NFL.(Stafford was a Parade All-American pick in 2005.) He set all the passing records for the Detroit Lions." On defense, Allen said, "Anthony Sleigel was the best defensive player. He started at Air Force and Ohio State as a linebacker. He played three years in the NFL. He is now the assistant strength coach for the football team at Ohio State."

He closed by assessing the 2014 Scot team. "For returners there is quarterback Brooks Burgin who has been offered a scholarship to Texas State. He was the district MVP and the Newcomer of the Year by the Dallas Morning News. Clayton Woods at center was All-District and has accepted an offer from UTSA. Jack Sides at offensive tackle was the Sophomore of the Year in district. Wide receiver Andrew Frost was All-District. Kevin Ken and Campbell Brooks, both IRs started part time. Offensive guard Rees LeMay made All-District. Carter

McDade is a running back with good hands and a shifty runner who started part time. Stephen Dieb, a running back who saw action in the playoffs is a tough physical runner. Outside linebacker Mitchell Kaufman has been offered by SMU and was an outstanding All-District player and on some All-State teams. Stephen Briggs started at strong safety while Boomer Backich started at free safety." About the Scots, Allen said, "The strength of our team is our senior leadership, offense and tradition. Our weakness is our needing experience on defense in the defensive line and cornerbacks.

THE HONDO OWLS

FIRST YEAR THEY PLAYED: 1912
ALL-TIME RECORD THROUGH 2013: 666-318-31
PERCENTAGE: 67.14%
PLAYOFF APPEARANCES: 48
STATE CHAMPIONSHIP GAMES LOST: 1956

Often the bridesmaid, but never the bride. That description might fit the Hondo Owls well. For Hondo has been to the playoffs more times among the teams featured in this book other than Highland Park, Amarillo and Plano. Despite a 6-4 record in 2012, Hondo had a rare miss in making the playoffs, which allowed Plano Senior High to tie the Owls in state playoff appearances. Ironically, in 2013 with the UIL allowing Class 3A schools to have four playoff teams from each district for the first time, Hondo would have kept that one-game lead over the Wildcats had the new rule been in effect for the 2012 season. In the last 15 years since 1999, the Owls have played in a Quarter-Final game three times and a Semi-Final game once. Going into the 2014 season, Highland Park had 55 appearances, Amarillo 52 and Hondo and Plano 48 each. So the "often the bridesmaid" title fits the Owls pretty well.

As to the "never the bride" description for Hondo, it is the only one of the 12 schools in *Friday's Winners* without a state championship title. The Owls did make it to the altar once in 1956 only to see Stinnett dash away their hopes for the 1A state crown with a 35-13 win. The Owls have advanced beyond the first round of the playoffs 26 times in their 102 year history of playing football.

There is more to Hondo's record than meets the eye. I discovered it in June of 2013 as I was searching for information on volleyball teams in Navarro County. I called Jerry Baldridge, the athletic director and head football coach at Rice High School for that information. In introducing myself, I mentioned to him that I was working on this book and the teams that were in it. He mentioned that he had been a coach at Hondo 20 years earlier. He actually joined the Owl coaching staff in 1988. What he told me next astounded me. Up to that point, Hondo had never fielded a seventh grade and eighth grade football team. The kids came into their freshmen year having had no football coaching to learn the basics until that point. What a load the Owls bore all those years before! It made their record number of playoff appearances before the new coaching staff began junior high football in 1988 all the more impressive. That amounted to their playoff appearances being done with one hand tied behind their back, an awesome achievement.

As I began to verify what Baldridge had told me, I was thinking that the entire 76 years that Hondo had been playing football had been accomplished without the benefit of their being a seventh and eighth grade program up to the year when Baldridge and his fellow coaches in 1988 started up junior high football. It turned out though, that sometime in the early 1960s, the Hondo ISD board of trustees had voted to stop the junior high program. There were several board members with medical backgrounds who had concerns about injuries to necks and knees who pushed for the halt.

I contacted former Hondo junior high physical education teacher and junior varsity coach Glen Schweers who explained to me how and why junior high football didn't exist in Hondo. But as he explained, it was a period of about 25 years. Instead of it being considered a disadvantage for the Owls, some of their rival coaches thought it was an advantage for the Owls as their teams were facing Hondo teams full of fresh and uninjured players. I told that to Quan Cosby, the great player for the Mart Panthers who went on to an outstanding career for the Texas Longhorns and then into the NFL and he responded, "I can see that. Facing players with fresh bodies ready for their first playing experience could be a disadvantage to some teams."

In addition to their stellar playoff and total games won records, the Owls have another asset going for them, their football stadium. J.D. Barry Field is named for their superintendent who served there from 1928 to 1942 and then from 1952 to 1971. With a seating capacity of 5880, Barry Field is one of the more picturesque stadiums in Texas. It is not constructed out of red brick giving it a college atmosphere aura like Highland Park's Highlander Stadium, but its walls are eye-catching as well as secure and sturdy. The walls are built from military landing strip panels called Marstin Matting plates which were created by the Sea Bees during World War II to create landing strips and roads quickly and easily for military units conducting their operations in remote areas lacking the infrastructure to easily allow planes and motor vehicles to operate in a normal manner. After the war, a lot of the landing strip panels became surplus material. Superintendent Barry saw the value and a different use in the eight foot long panels which could be joined together by metal tabs. Each panel has three rows of strips of holes about the size of big coffee cups, 28 holes to a row. The holes allow the viewer to see through into the field at the different height levels they are placed. It sorta reminded me of the ultimate version of the knotholes in the fences at baseball fields through which kids used to watch the games. A chance for all passersby to be members of the Knothole Gang.

The Hondo ISD bought enough of the panels to build its stadium. The entire stadium is surrounded by these panels to an approximate height of 10 feet. It has to be seen to discover what an ingenious idea it was to construct a football stadium from these surplus military plane landing strips; when the Air Force used them, they laid them down on bare earth to create a solid surface for the planes to roll on. They only wanted to put the planes in the air from the landing strips. Probably never thought they could put the strips up in the air erect and joined together to create the unique walls that surround Barry Field.

But it's not just the landing strips that make Barry Field one of the better places to attend a Friday night game. There is a closeness to the field for viewers in the stands because there is not a track around the field. The football field is about 20 feet away from the stands on both sides. It used to be even closer until injuries to some players caused by being too close to the low fences on plays where they were forced out of bounds caused the school board to get the stadium seating moved back about 10 feet on both sides for the players' protection.

Then there are the oak trees on both ends of the football field. They are pretty to look at, but they also sometimes play a part in the games. They are trimmed enough not to protrude out over the field, but there have been times when a team kicking an extra point or a field goal has had the ball lodge in the branches of the trees. That is most likely to happen on the north end zone as there is an area created behind the south end zone before the trees there and the concession stand for overflow crowds to stand 10 people deep to watch the game. Artificial turf was installed in Barry Field in 2006 which took away one of the things that made it a unique place to play a game. The field had to be leveled by the dirt contractors to lay the turf down. It was discovered that the south end zone portion of the field was three feet lower than the north end. Imagine losing the coin flip to where your team had to being going north in the fourth quarter, uphill, tired, sore and hot from the intense South Texas heat, especially in the early part of the season that begins in late August.

A couple of more observations about the field were also gained on my trip there on July 23, 2014. Just like Highland Park, the Hondo campus is landlocked. But I understand that should the need to expand the seating capacity in Barry Field ever happen, the school district has the right to extend the seating overhead out above the street. Furthermore, you have to admire the eye for value that exists in the fans of Hondo High School. You might even say they have a knack for making lemonade from the so-called lemons that come their way from time to time. Case in point: Hondo had a home game on October 12, 2001, which was called because of an approaching tornado with Hondo leading Poteet 41-0. The officials didn't want the fans to be caught out in the high winds coming their way. That was a good decision as some big branches on the oak trees on both ends of the field were knocked down in the storm. The press box was damaged when the tornado hit. Luckily, there were no injuries. The branches had to be cleared away and disposed of, But quick thinking Doc Zerr, who you will know more about in some later paragraphs, suggested to the powers that be not to pick up the limbs and run them through a mulching machine. Instead, he suggested that the limbs be cut into one inch thick pieces and turned into mementos for Owl fans. The building construction class took charge of the project and created owls, footballs and lyres for the band members out of the wood pieces. They sanded them and buffed them as keepsakes. The Hondo Booster Club sold the wooden mementoes to Owl boosters. The booster club netted around $70,000.00 out of the downed limbs as a result.

There were several players from the late 50s-early 60s era who really stood out in their play for the Owls. The first on the list is George L. Brucks, a guard and linebacker on the 1957, 1958 and 1959 teams. In his first two seasons, the Owls were rebuilding having lost many players who played for the State Championship in 1956. So those two teams didn't make it to the playoffs. In 1959, his senior year, the Owls won the district crown again beating San Felipe-Del Rio 20-14. They lost the Bi-District game to Freer 13-6.

Brucks reflected on his days playing for Hondo, "People in Hondo love football. In the 1959 game against San Felipe, Sidney Blanks and I were kicked out of the game for fighting. Hondo won." Brucks was an all-district selection each year for Hondo. In his first two years, he was coached by Buck Carver, who had a great five year run as the Owls coach with a 41-15-4 mark. In his senior year, Joe Scott coached the Owls. After Hondo, Brucks played for Texas including the 1963 National Champion team. One of his teammates at Texas was Gene Gifford who played for the Amarillo Sandies on that 1957 team. When I told him I was interviewing Brucks for this book, Gifford remarked, "Brucks is one of the toughest guys I ever played with." Today he is back in Hondo as the owner of Brucks Insurance where, as he says, "I support the local sports including football."

John Zeer, who most people in Hondo and San Antonio call Doc, has been a great supporter of Owl football in addition to having played on the varsity in 1958, '59, '60 and '61. He was a linebacker and offensive guard earning All-District honors at both positions for his junior and senior years. While he played, Hondo advanced to the Bi-District game only once in 1959 and lost it to Freer 13-6. A severe head injury that landed him in the hospital for several touch and go days ended his football playing days. One of his coaches pointed him in the direction of becoming an athletic trainer. Zeer had three different coaches during his time on the team-Max Carver in 1958, Joe Scott in 1959 and Doug Johnson in 1960 and 1961.

Doc commented about playing in Hondo, "It is expected especially if your father or brother played before you." Zeer's family is a five generation family of Hondo players featured in my chapter, Football, a Family Tradition. In talking about the most significant game he played in, he said, "In 1960, both Hondo and Devine were ranked in the top 5 of Texas. We lost our quarterback in the first half and lost the game 18-6. Devine continued and lost in the State Semi-Finals to the eventual state champion."

After getting his certification as an athletic trainer, he served in different markets for a number of years. He had signed on to be a trainer for schools in the north side of San Antonio when he met Emory Ballard as he coached at San Angelo Central. Bellard was impressed enough with him that he contacted his bosses in San Antonio to get permission to approach him about the San Angelo trainer position. He offered him a substantial increase in salary to come west which he did for three years beginning in 1966. Eventually he came back to Hondo to become the Owls athletic trainer from 1972 through 1988. He had developed such extensive knowledge about orthopedic injuries that he became a consultant to a number of orthopedic surgeons. He invented and got patents on orthopedic braces for ankles, knees and elbows. He became the national sales manager for Texas Orthopedic Products, retiring in 2009.

Today he is back in Hondo where he says, "I continue to support Hondo athletics both morally and financially." All along he has bought the season football tickets for the same seats that his parents began buying in 1947. That's 67 years of one family getting the same tickets year after year.

An Owl who played during Hondo's most recent deepest run in the state playoffs is Wes Favor. He was on the Hondo varsity for four years, 2004 through 2007. Wes played middle linebacker, fullback and running back in his four years. His team didn't make the playoffs when he was a freshman. In 2005, Hondo went three rounds deep making the Regional Semi-Finals and ending the year with an 8-5 record. The Owls in 2006 started the year with 14 straight wins losing out in the State Semi-Finals to Liberty Hill 19-35. His senior year, the Owls went to Bi-District and finished the year with an 8-3 record.

Favor got some recognition for his play gaining second team All-District honors as a sophomore. When Hondo made it to the State Semi-Finals, he was named first team All-District, second team all greater San Antonio area, first team All-SW Texas and honorable mention All-State. A torn ACL he suffered before getting to district play in 2007, his senior year, caused him to play a few games wearing a brace. He was selected second team All-District. He walked on to play at Texas A & M-Kingsville, but the torn ACL kept coming back so he gave up football.

He has many special memories of playing for Hondo which he expressed in a letter to me. Favor began, "I feel honored to have played for the Hondo Owls. What makes Hondo so special and successful is the pride each player feels when he straps on a helmet with a "H" on the side of it and suit up in their Blue & White jersey. Pride and tradition is the key to Hondo's success. Each generation lays a path of ambition and competition for future players. Each player knows the success of the former players and strives to be better. Growing up, my teammates and I looked up to the prior players like they were heroes; we all agreed we would strive to be better. After leaving, we all try to impose a strong positive attitude toward school pride. We persuade future players that this is the best town in Texas to play football, which is an ongoing tradition for all Hondo players. Also, our community and fans make the Hondo football program special through our support and attendance at the games."

He continues,"In the four years I played for Hondo, P. J. Wells was the head coach. He was persistent in his goals for success. He was confident in the program he ran which made it easy for his players to believe in him. He also surrounded himself with a successful qualified staff: Jeff Rochat, Jeff Stivors, George Proctor, Joe Ortega, Peter Perez, Cy Barr and Tim Williams to name a few."

About playing, Favor said, "The best district game that I remember was in 2006 when we met up with Devine in the final game of district play. Both teams had a record of 9-0, and there was no other team the Hondo Owls enjoy defeating more. There were so many fans in attendance from both towns that the stands and all surface area around the track was completely full. It is impossible to describe the intensity of the atmosphere. The sight of endless encouraging fans and thundering cheers were surreal from a player's standpoint. The

Owls won the game 38-13, but had a tough fight. Every year, the competiveness between the towns is the same."

He recalled some special playoff games, "Many playoff games stand out in my memory, but beating Wimberley in the 2006 Regional finals at the Alamo Dome was pretty impressive. Wimberley beat us the year before in the third round of the playoffs and went on to win the State Championship. We were ramped up for revenge going into this game. At the end of the first quarter, we were down 21-0. We dug deep and pulled out a 42-35 victory. There was not one single play or series that can be attributed to the reason for the 'turnaround.' We all knew what we wanted and knew what had to do to win. Our record was 14-0 after that game, which is the best record any Hondo football team has had in the school's history."

Two years ago, the Hondo ISD Board of Trustees selected Jeff Rochat to be the athletic director and head football coach. In doing so, they brought in one of their former players who lives and breathes the Owl legacy and is ready to pass it on to his players. If the UIL allowed coaches to go recruit players for their football teams, Rochat would be one of the first ones pitching to prospects about what makes Honda football a unique lifetime experience. He gave a sample of his enthusiasm as he answered the first of several questions I had for him. He said, "The special thing about Hondo is the record number of playoff appearances. Over 100 years of football, the historic football stadium. I played for the Owls in the 80s so it is really special to get the opportunity to coach the Owls."

About his own career as an Owl, Rochat was on the varsity three years, 1983-1985. He played outside linebacker, free safety, wide receiver and wing back. In his sophomore year, Hondo had a 12-2 record. They lost to Sweeny in the State Quarter-Finals 14-6. The Owls went 8-3 in his junior year and 5-5 his senior year.

Next I asked him about the football games he considered to be exciting wins since he began coaching at his alma mater in 2012. "In my two short years as the head coach, we have had several exciting wins. The first one that comes to mind was in 2012 versus Somerset. We were down 16-10 with minutes to go. We scored and made the extra point to go up 17-16. On the next series they scored on a 90 yard bomb to go up 22-17. We then take the ball and complete two passes to their 30 yard line. On the next play, our quarterback, Zane Carroll, scrambles for 30 yards for the score with two seconds left on the clock. We kick off and hold them winning the game 23-22."

He continued,"The next one was in 2013. Down to our district rival Devine at Devine 14-0 with under three minutes to play. We came roaring back and tied the game to go into OT. We scored first in OT, but missed the extra point. We then recovered a fumble on their third play from scrimmage to win the game 20-14."

"But the best Hondo game I have ever been a part of occurred in 2006. I was the defensive coordinator for the Hondo team that went to the State Semi-Finals, losing to state champion Liberty Hill. (The loss score was 35-19.) We played Wimberley in the Quarter-Finals in the Alamo Dome. They had beaten us the year before something like 54-8. (actually 52-8 in the Quarter-Finals) They exploded for a 21-0 lead, but we came back to tie the game at the half 21-21. We held on for a 42-35 win. P.J. Wells (now an assistant at San Antonio Madison) was the head coach."

Rochat continued telling about a game that had a sour ending, "In 2012, we played Devine in Week 10. They were already in the playoffs. If we won the game, we were the district champions. If we lost, we were out on tiebreakers. IT WAS HONDO'S 1000TH FOOTBALL GAME. We are winning 10-7 with about two and one-half minutes to play. We forced them to punt on their own 45 yard line. They shift before they punt and we adjust and no one jumps. A flag comes from the umpire and we get called for an unsportsmanlike conduct call for disconcerting signals. It's a five yard penalty, but they mark off 15 and give them a first down. They march down and score with under five seconds to play to win the game 14-10. Needless to say, the crew was split up and sanctioned, but the result stood. A heartbreaking loss in my first year as the Owls head coach. In this first two years, I have only coached one playoff game, a loss to Rockport Fulton in Bi-District this year."

When it came to naming players who have stood out to him, Rochat replied, "In 2006, Andy Werner was our running back. He had over 2000 yards and scored 30 TD's. He also kicked 18 of 22 extra point attempts and was four of four on field goals. He was also an outstanding safety. He is the best offensive player I have ever coached. He was tough, fast, strong and a fierce competitor. In that same year, Wes Favor, our inside linebacker, was the best defensive player I have ever coached. He was a true leader, physical, smart and relentless on defense."

As for the 2014 season, he says, "We have drawn a tough district. We are with Lytle, Wimberley, Navarro and Llano. Lytle won our district last year and has some very good players coming back, but they had a late coaching change. Wimberley is a traditional power and is picked to win the district. Navarro is always good and well coached. Llano made the playoffs as well last year. It will be a dog fight, every week. I could see us winning the district just as easily as being the one left out. We will have to coach well and our players will need to stay healthy and compete (they always compete hard and never quit). Our strengths are our skill kids and defense. We are rebuilding our offensive line so that is my biggest concern."

THE LONGVIEW LOBOS

FIRST YEAR THEY PLAYED: 1909
ALL-TIME RECORD THROUGH 2013: 668-332-53
PERCENTAGE: 65.95%
PLAYOFF APPEARANCES: 39
STATE CHAMPIONSHIP GAMES WON: 1937
STATE CHAMPIONSHIP GAMES LOST: 1997, 2008, 2009

It's been seventy-seven years since the Longview Lobos posted a new state champion banner up on their wall, but with three appearances in the last seventeen years in the state finals, it just seems to be a matter of time before the fans of the Green and White will see it happen again. When you realize that the Lobo coach John King has won over eighty per cent of the games he's coached there and see the quality of players that King and his assistant coaches work with each year, you start to become a believer. The fan support is as strong an asset as almost any other school in Texas. That is illustrated by the story of just one fan, Ralph Bailey. He has been buying season tickets since 1949. That's sixty four years and growing. And he estimates that he has only missed three or four home games in that stretch of time. Until his wife of sixty-seven years, Melba, suffered a stroke that has kept her homebound the past two years, he nearly had a streak going like that for the Lobo road games. Melba even accompanied him on a lot of those road trips to cheer on their beloved Lobos. Now for the home games when he has someone to take care of Melba, his son David Bailey goes with him. Bailey, who is ninety one, says he buys up to eleven season tickets each year. He keeps two for himself and distributes the rest to other family members and friends.

In a visit to Longview on September 5, 2014, to the Lobos' game with visiting Tyler John Tyler, I found another Lobo fan who began purchasing season tickets a year earlier than Bailey, in 1948. Jean and Tillman Perkins began buying the tickets and attending games together until he passed away eight years ago. Jean has kept buying the season tickets, the family tradition uninterrupted for sixty-six years. She now attends games with her daughter as she says, "I love football games." Her daughter is Pam Taylor who is married to Brent Taylor. He has his own record of longevity going as the radio voice of the Lobos on KOOI, Sunni 106.5. He has been at the job since the 1977 season, thirty-seven years of broadcasting Longview football throughout East Texas.

Jean and I were getting acquainted in the press box at Lobo Stadium, one of the prettiest stadiums among those I have seen at the schools in *Friday's Winners*. It was built and opened in October 1976 and updated since then with the latest bells and whistles that make up the state of the art in today's football facilities. Lobo Stadium has an instant replay scoreboard and chair back seats on the home side of the field. There is capacity for 9,215 fans should there be a big game against a long term rival like Lufkin, Tyler John Tyler or Marshall. In the center of the field is the Rockin' L logo, a distinctive mark of the Lobos. The WOW! factor for me is the drive east on Hawkins Parkway going past the high school complex where, all of a sudden, the stadium is open like a bowl on that one end where the driver going past is eyeball to eyeball with players and band members on the field. Add to that impression the fact that there are a number of tall pine trees between Hawkins Parkway and the end of the playing field and surrounding track and it's a brief, but breathtaking view, worth circling around to see if there is an opportunity to go by a little more slowly and drink in the sight of this beautiful structure with the natural scenery enhancing the view. At this point, there is a pedestrian bridge that crosses over Hawkins Parkway to the high school's athletic facilities across from the stadium. That includes tennis courts, softball fields and baseball fields. Very impressive. Try to be there when the daily traffic is at its lightest as you drive east to get the full effect. I don't know when that is, but it will be worth your time to see it.

It seems to be a regular pattern for each of these schools to have long periods of time when playoff appearances are rare. In the case of Longview, the Lobos made about eight playoff appearances between the years 1924 and 1942. Then things got sparse for them. They won district in 1947 and got to go to the playoffs. It would be twenty years before that happened again. The Lobos tied for the championship in 1958 and 1959, but weren't the district representative to the playoffs. During this stretch of missing the playoffs, two of the best players in Lobo history were on the team at different times. Linebacker Loyd Phillips played from 1960 through 1962. Then quarterback James Street, a four-sport athlete for the Lobos, played from 1963 through 1965. In their combined six years playing for Longview, the best records achieved by the team was 5-5 several times. The Lobos had several losing seasons during this stretch. Yet, when they got to college, both Phillips and Street became some of the greatest players ever leading their respective schools, Arkansas and Texas. They both were selected to the Texas High School Sports Hall of Fame.

The player who ultimately helped Longview get to the playoffs for the first time in 20 years was Steve Judy. He played quarterback behind Street in 1965, his sophomore year and Street's senior year. He started his last two seasons and won several honors for his play. He was All-District in 1966 and 1967. He was also All East Texas both years. He was the District MVP in 1967. His big honor was being chosen to the Prep All-American football team as a senior. Judy discussed his years on the Lobos in the following interview. He began, "It is a special experience to be able to play for the Lobos, because of the long tradition and to represent the city of Longview. I had two different head coaches during this time. Ty Bain was head coach my sophomore and junior years and Tommy Hudspeth my senior year. I really enjoyed playing for both, but they were different in their style of coaching. Coach Bain was a more hard-nosed coach whereas Coach Hudspeth was a little more laid back. Both were great coaches in their own way."

I asked him about some of the big games he was in and Judy replied, "The most significant district game I played in was the last regular season game at Lufkin in 1967. We were 9-0 and still had to win this game to make the playoffs. Lufkin had lost only district game so the winner advanced to Bi-District. We fell behind 14-0 very quickly and were down at the half. With a great team effort, we came away with the biggest win for Longview in a long time. Longview had not advanced to the playoffs in twenty years (1947). I was able to contribute to the win by running for four touchdowns."

Judy continued about their experience in the Bi-District game, "We advanced to Bi-District against the Richardson Eagles and played at Lobo Stadium. Again this was the first Bi-District game for us in twenty years and obviously the first Bi-District game in Lobo Stadium in 20 years. We finished the regular season 10-0 and ranked number two in the state behind an Abilene Cooper team led by quarterback Jack Mildren. Unfortunately, this was a game that nothing went our way. We had a field goal attempt blocked and run back for a touchdown, but still led 13-6 at the half. In the second half, Richardson drove for a touchdown and since we were ahead on penetrations 3-1, they decided to go for two. They tried a quick pass to the tight end, but it bounced off his hands and fell into the arms of their fullback who had faked a dive through the line and was laying on his back when the ball landed on him. Behind 14-13 late in the fourth quarter, we forced a punt in hopes to get the ball and drive for at least a game winning field goal. Our returner mistakenly tried to field the punt inside our 10 yard line and fumbled. Richardson recovered on the one and ran in for a touchdown and beat us. Final score 21-13."

I asked him about his involvement today with the Lobos and he replied, "I have not been too much involved as I have gotten older. I was more involved when my two sons played for the Lobos. I was the Lobo Booster Club president during those years."

Judy played for TCU after he graduated from Longview High. Today he is a stockbroker with Wells Fargo Advisers in Longview.

That same night of September 5, 2014, when I was there, Doug Cox was honored at halftime on the field for his accomplishments as a competitive coach for Longview in the rivalry with Tyler. In fourteen years, he coached the Lobos to a 120-34-4 record. In his second year in 1975, the Lobos made it all the way to the State Semi-Finals. In his next to last year, 1986, he took the Lobos to the State Quarter-Finals. So his best season was 1975, when the Lobos finished with a record of 13-1-0. In his 14 years, there were three other seasons with 10 wins and five years with nine wins. He never even had just a .500 season, a pretty outstanding career.

It took the setting of a state record to stop Longview's drive to playing for the State Championship in 1975. Coach Cox had his team rolling in the playoffs. A Bi-District win over Plano 26-0 avenged a 28-21 loss to the Wildcats in 1974. In the Regional game, the Lobos beat Conroe by a missed extra point 14-13. In the Quarter-Finals, Dallas Carter fell to the Lobos 21-7. Odessa Permian was their Semi-Final opponent. In the first quarter of that game, Permian's Russell Wheatley kicked a sixty-two yard field goal for a new state record. Permian held on to beat Longview 10-9. Wheatley's record still stands, but has been matched by two others, David Leaverton of Midland High in 1995, ironically against Permian, and by Ralph Heaten of El Paso Irvin against El Paso Bowie in 1992.

Cox had some comments on his coaching career with the Lobos. How it even happened is an interesting story in itself. He said, "I was coaching with Clint Humphrey in San Antonio and he decided to try for the job as head coach at Spring Branch which he got. I was one of three coaches who went with him there. But after a year, he was ready to move again, this time to one of two jobs open, either the head coaching job in Odessa or the head coaching job in Longview. He ended up in Longview and asked if I wanted to move with him again. I said yes and we started out camping out in the gym until we arranged for housing so we could move our families here."

He continued, "That first year in 1971 was spent putting our system into place. The Lobos went 3-6-1 for the season. It was much better in 1972 as we made it to the playoffs going out in the first round with a 10-1-0 record. In

1973, the Lobos finished 8-2-0 and Coach Humphrey was ready to move again. I wanted to stay here and applied for the head coaching job which I got.

I asked him about what other games besides the 13-0 string in 1975 had really had an impact on him. He quickly replied, "My first year as head coach, we met Tyler John Tyler late in the district schedule. The Lions were defending State Champions and had nine defensive starters back including Earl Campbell's two younger brothers. They were ranked number one in the state. Our team averaged about 178 pounds per player while their players were about 100 pounds heavier. We were both 8-0 when we played. Our players played about half a step faster than the Lions. It made the difference. The effort that my kids made was superb, they wouldn't be denied. I had a picture that illustrated that. It was of the Lion runner trying to get the yardage on a fourth and one play. The picture showed all eleven Lobo helmets on that Tyler runner. We won the game 29-7. It was the best coaching night of my career."

One of the players he had inherited from Coach Humphrey was his quarterback, Steve Gaddis. Cox stated he was a great leader. I interviewed Gaddis asking the same questions I've asked every other player in *Friday's Winners*. One of them is how did your team advance in the playoffs each year you were on the varsity. He answered about the 1973 season with two words, "Earl Campbell." Tyler John Tyler was in their district and went undefeated as the Lions won state with the "Tyler Rose" leading the way. He found playing for the Lobos to be a special experience because of the Lobo pride and tradition. He had both coaches leading him as indicated above. About Coaches Humphreys and Cox, he said, "I loved them both. They taught mental toughness. Boot Camp days were tough!"

Asked what district game stood out the most to him, Gaddis replied, "It was the John Tyler game in 1974. It was number one versus number two. There was no school that day. There was a send off pep rally that lined the streets as we left Longview. Those are special memories for me." Longview as mentioned by Coach Cox beat Tyler 29-7 that day.

Gaddis moved on to a coaching career after college. He began at Cameron Yoe as an offensive and defensive ends coach from 1980 through 1982. He was on Toby York's staff that led the Yoemen to their first State Championship in 1981. He says that State Championship game was the biggest one he has been a part of coaching. He joined Cox on the Lobo staff from 1983 through 1988. He also coached the defensive and offensive ends for the Lobos. He got his chance to be a head coach in 1989 taking over at Tyler Spring Hill. He coached there for six years before moving to Hallsville for three years. Then he came back to Spring Hill for an additional seven years. He ended his coaching career with a four year stint at Lewisville. For the twenty years he led teams, Gaddis compiled a record of 129-88-1. Today he is retired living in Georgia to be closer to his grandchildren.

Cox also mentioned that a great player on defense that he coached was Henry Williams, a defensive end on the 1975 team. Williams went to Texas on a football scholarship after he graduated. Another player he mentioned was his son, Brad. Brad was selected for the Mean Green, a select group of sixteen Lobos considered the toughest kids on the team. He was on the 1986 team that beat Waco High in Bi-District 25-19 and Highland Park 41-14 in Regional. They lost in the Quarter-Finals to Plano 17-12. Another player who stood out to Cox was Leo McCoy, a tailback on the 1974-75 teams. He had over two hundred carries in his senior year and never fumbled the ball. On defense was Hosea Taylor, a defensive tackle who played on the 1974, 1975 and 1976 teams. Taylor stood 6'5" and weighed 280 pounds. He was athletic enough that he played well on the basketball court, dunking the ball with authority. As was mentioned in the Recognition chapter, he represented Longview in the 1977 High School Coaches All-Star Game.

Two other games Cox mentioned were back to back non-district games in 1986 and 1987 with Dallas Carter. The Lobos lost in 1986 to Carter 19-0. In 1987, the Lobos edged the Cowboys 10-7.

Shortly after Cox took the helm at Longview, he instituted a pledge program for the players which players from thirty years ago still talk to him about it today. The idea came to him from hearing Freddie Steinmark, the University of Texas star who had his leg amputated after contracting bone cancer. Steinmark, who grew up in the Denver, Colorado area, played on the team called the Rough Riders. Asked how he handled this terrible change in his life, Steinmark said that he would recite the pledge created for the Rough Riders to help them handle the misfortunes in their lives that affected how they played football. Each of the Lobos, players and coaches, had to stand up before their teammates and coaches and recite the pledge. Afterwards, the player would be given a medallion to wear and remind them of the pledge they each had memorized. Below is the pledge.

> As a Longview Lobo, I will never quit or accept defeat. I will always put my team and its goals ahead of myself. When the going gets tough and my determination weakens, I will rededicate myself and throw more into my efforts. The most important part of football is to always have courage and play aggressively as a unit.
>
> I, _____, pledge on my honor to uphold the tradition that other Lobos before me have worked so hard to establish. Thumbs up for the Green!

John King became the head coach at Longview in 2004. He has compiled one of the most impressive coaching records in Texas since then. He has led the Lobos to a 112-24-0 record through 2013. That is a winning percentage of 82.352 per cent for that ten year run. He joined the Lobo coaching staff in 2000 before assuming the top role after four years. In his ten years, King has grasped what Lobo football and tradition is all about. He expressed those thoughts in an early July 2014 interview before moving on to discuss memorable games for the Lobos in the past ten years, his take on the top players to wear the green and white during his regime and to assess the Lobos' chances in the 2014 season. He began, "Longview is a 'one horse' town and the Lobo Nation loves their football. Folks in Longview live for their Friday night football and season ticket holders date back to the 40s and 50s. Season tickets are part of divorce settlements and living wills. The pride of being a Lobo is handed down from generation to generation. YOU ARE EXPECTED TO WIN REGARDLESS OF THE SITUATION."

He detailed eight games played over the past twelve years that were especially meaningful to him and his teams. He began with 2001, "The Lobos defeat three-time State Champion Midland Lee 33-17. This started our turnaround with a new staff. In 2002, the Lobos won 31-28 to knock off #1 nationally ranked Evangel Christian. Then in 2008, in the State Quarter-Finals, we beat Waco Midway 43-42 on a two point conversion in overtime to advance to the State Semi-Finals. In 2009, we beat Allen 28-25 after trailing 17-0 at half time."

King went on about the biggest district games during his coaching time with the Lobos. "In 2005, in week ten, we beat Tyler John Tyler 42-13 with approximately 15,000 in attendance. Then in 2011, also in week ten, we met DeSoto in a game televised on Fox Sports Southwest. The Lobos won 23-21 on a safety late in the game to win our eighth consecutive district title (a school record)." Finally King stated that the two 4A State Championship games in 2008 and 2009, both against Lake Travis, were the biggest playoff games the Lobos have been in since he took the reins in 2004. Lake Travis won both contests as part of their string of five consecutive State Championships.

A number of players made his list of top offensive players that he has coached. He started with Malcolm Kelly, a wide receiver in 2004. "He was a big play guy— just get it close and he'll catch it." In 2005, it was tailback Vondrell McGee- 'vision and burst,' fullback Chris Ivory 'the Hammer' brought the wood as a blocker and runner - great hands, and offensive lineman Trent Williams-the best player I've ever coached, strength, balance, nasty. In the 2009 run to the state championship game, King said, "athlete/quarterback Aaron Johnson was 'A LEADER & WINNER !!!!!!!!!!!', offensive lineman Bryce

Redman was ' the toughest player I've ever coached - stomped out a sprained ankle for two quarters in the third playoff game - returned to play in the fourth - you would have to cut his head off to stop him and tailback Tyler McCray-just get him the ball and let him spin." In 2010 he cited wr/qb Peter Robinson, "He could do it all—wr/te/qb/ss/lb." The cupboard wasn't bare in 2013 as he mentioned junior tailback Jamycal Hasty, "The total package—runner, receiver, kick returner-can even play quarterback."

Longview is not without some defensive standouts also. King mentions, "2001: Willie Andrews- defensive back, running back, kick returner-could do it all. Played strong safety in college and the pros. 2003: Linebacker Robert Henson-a wild banshee who loved to practice and play the game. 2000: linebacker Marvin Byrdsong - great range and speed. 2012: strong safety/free safety Corey Bartley—'our Honey Badger'—made plays all over the field. 2009: defensive lineman Bubba Vactor—the man in the middle. 2013: strong safety—similar to Andrews—could do it all. Ss/olb/cb/kr—great team player—great student as well."

Finally King was enthusiastic about the 2014 season, "It should be another good year for the Lobos. We lost 37 seniors from the 2013 team. But we have a good nucleus of returning starters and lettermen. The strength of the team should be at the running back position with the return of Jamycal Hasty (an early Baylor commit) and Marquise Hunter. Add in Tyler Miller and Austin Moore. The offensive line will be above average with the tackle/tight end spots being our strengths. The defensive secondary should be a strong part as well. Our weakness is depth in the defensive line and inexperience at receiver and linebacker."

THE MART PANTHERS

FIRST YEAR THEY PLAYED: 1912
ALL-TIME RECORD THROUGH 2013: 701-347-42
PERCENTAGE: 66.23%
PLAYOFF APPEARANCES: 44
STATE CHAMPIONSHIP GAMES WON: 1957, 1969, 1999, 2006, 2010
STATE CHAMPIONSHIP GAMES LOST: 1986, 2000, 2008, 2012

Just how much of an impact can a Class 2A school, with an enrollment of fewer than 175 students, have in the all time winningest football programs in Texas when compared to the giant 6A and 5A schools it is linked with? Ask yourself, have any of those bigger schools had the top pick in the 2012 NFL draft in their weight rooms on a hot Saturday, June 23, 2012, holding a press conference for all the local television sports reporters from within a 100 mile radius? This right after he spent three hours on the football field throwing passes to youngsters as young as six years old, timing them in 40 yard runs and delivering life lesson talks to a rapt audience of 300 of these young campers? How many of the big schools had the Baylor University cheerleaders out on the field leading 25 young cheerleaders in getting the fans in the packed stands yelling for the home team, and not the Bears? How many of those big schools had a number of current NFL players and former college stars from a variety of colleges, but mainly from the University of Texas, down on the field working to teach those 300 campers fundamentals of football, volunteering their time to do this for free? The obvious answer to these loaded questions is NONE of them. But little Mart High School, the smallest member of our featured schools could answer YES to all the above questions. It was there on that Saturday that Andrew Luck, late of the Stanford Cardinal, two –time runner-up as the winner of the Heisman Trophy, and recently the top pick in the

NFL's 2012 draft volunteered his time to work with the 300 campers attending Quan Cosby's Fourth Annual football camp.

After the Indianapolis Colts drafted him to replace the legendary Peyton Manning who they turned loose after 13 fabulous seasons, Luck became a teammate of Cosby, a wide receiver and kick returner for the Colts. Cosby also happened to first be a Mart Panther, leading the 1999 team to the AA State Championship. Cosby happened to wear the number 12 on his Colts jersey, Luck's number at Stanford. It is customary for a rookie of Luck's prominence wanting to get his number back from a teammate to pay cash for it. Cosby offered the number 12 to Luck provided he help out at the camp on the Mart football field. The offer was accepted, the promise kept and the Mart star became #14 for the Colts' upcoming season.

One thing about Mart is that decade after decade, the Panthers manage to come up with a string of wins that makes them contenders to go deep into the playoffs. It keeps the home folks happy and content and it works in favor of the players to get looks from college recruiters on a regular basis. It is the Mart tradition and it is carried on by the coaches as well as the players. One such player that benefitted from a run in the late 50's is Jerry Hopkins. It is his name that pops up the most when the discussion is on players who made an impact in winning their first State Championship in 1957. That was his junior year and Mart had a 14-0-1 record when it was over. The tie came in the state championship game, 7-7 with White Oak. Today, there are no ties, only overtime periods to keep going until one team prevails.

Hopkins played for Mart in 1956, 1957 and 1958. He was a right guard on offense and a linebacker on defense. Mart's win loss record during his years on the varsity are records that virtually all high school football players wish their schools accomplished when they played. Mart went to the Quarter-Finals in 1956 and in 1958. Those years, the Panthers had very respectable 11-2-0 records. In 1957, Mart was undefeated at 14-0-0 going into the State Championship game with White Oak. Jerry talked about how that game turned out, "We were ahead on penetrations and first downs, but the score was tied 7-7. We thought we had won, but there was an agreement made before the game that a tie would result in co-champions. Our team was devastated because we thought we had won." He talked about a district game that was memorable for him, "In the 1958 Franklin game, I kicked for an extra point, but after the ball went through the goal post as good, the ball hit a tree on the outside perimeter of the field, bounced back through the uprights onto the field and an official ruled it no good." It was a memorable play, but not the result he wanted. When he walked off the field for Mart as a player for the final time, Hopkins had played in 36 wins, four losses and one tie and never got stopped short of the State Quarter-Finals. He was selected a Super Centex player by the Waco Tribune-Herald for all three years of 1956, 1957 and 1958. He was voted All-State for his play in 1957 and 1958.

His coach for all three years was Clifford "Cotton" Lindhoff. Hopkins stated, "Coach Lindhoff expected perfection." With Hopkins and the other players in his class, that 36-4-1 mark in three years is as close as he came to reaching it. Lindhoff coached four other seasons for the Panthers, in 1955 and 1959, 1960 and 1961. His record for those years without Hopkins and crew was 23-18-1. Hopkins received a scholarship to play college football at Texas A & M.

He closed with comments about the Mart winning record and what he does to encourage it to continue to move forward, "The tradition of winning makes playing football in Mart a special experience. When I am asked, I tell the kids to work to maintain the winning tradition."

Twelve years after the Panthers grabbed their first State Championship in 1957 against White Oak, it was time to get number two. Leading the way for coach Edd Burleson with his play on the field was the Panther quarterback Calvin Jones, Jr. He had a fabulous career on the Mart varsity in 1968-69-70. The teams he was on lost only one game when he was under the center taking the snaps. He commented on how it was playing for Mart starting in grade school; "I lost one football game in my high school career, it was the last one against Rosebud-Lott. I called my own plays in those days, the first and last plays I called were touchdown passes."

He talked about Mart, "Mart is a small town and the only thing in your life was church, school and playing something. We played football the year round. I learned about football from David Byrd, a friend of the family. Started drawing my own plays in the first grade on a Big Chief tablet. I had an offense ready for any neighborhood or grade school game. In sixth grade, Coach Burleson called us together during PE and put together an offense and defense. The very first play I called in organized school football went for a touchdown with Jimmy Bevers getting the call on a double reverse to fake out Mike Ward in the sixth grade. I love my high school coach. He will be 80 on September 2. I spent more time with him growing up than I did my dad. He was my Friend, Coach, Sunday School Teacher and someone I really looked up to. I felt he could get the best out of us no matter what the game. I really remember the times when he wanted to make you feel special, you could run through a brick wall when he got you up."

Jones continued on about playing for the Panthers, "My best called district game was against Buffalo. We won 57-0 and ran up 725 yards of offense. We got our scouting report against Groesbeck after the Buffalo game. Groesbeck, a big rival in 1969, held us scoreless in the first half, but we scored 33 points in the second half to win our first district championship since 1965.

Randy Hyden, who played for Groesbeck, who now lives in Teague, met with me after the game at midfield. He told me we could win it all. That was the first time I thought about a State Championship. We were grade school buddies and classmates. He came over to my house and told me he was moving to Groesbeck in eighth grade and cried in our garage when he told me.

I called good games in the playoffs, but in the Quarter-Final game, against White Oak, we played the #1 ranked team in Texas and it was played in Athens in the Mud Bowl. It must have rained six inches that day starting early in the morning. We kicked off to White Oak and they scored their only touchdown in four plays. Louis Thornton scored in the second quarter on a one yard blast. I was the only guy on the field whose number you could make out. My white uniform was still clean in the fourth quarter because I never got hit. Everything went perfect on our 54 yard drive to victory. No fumbles, great blocking and we just ran it down their throat. I scored on a one yard plunge when I noticed no one was paying attention to anything I did. I even landed on top of my center Bud Chadwell and guard David Connally, I scored four times that year. Every time I carried the ball, I scored a touchdown. I have yet to gain over a yard.

I felt the football team of 1970 was even better than the 1969 team, but we only went 9-1 and lost the last game. When you lost the last game, you didn't make the playoffs in those days. After graduation I watched my brothers play. Brother Keith, who played at Baylor, was beaten out by Mike Singletary. Brother Neil wore my old numbers when he played."

Life after football for Jones is all about continuing to support Mart's highly successful program. Jones says, "I always promoted Mart and Mart football. I ran the chain for a number of years at most home games. I served on the school board for 12 years. I was even elected Mayor and served 2007 to 2009.

The night before the 2006 State Championship, I helped organize a pancake supper for the team. We had former coaches Kemp and Lindloff and Jerry Hopkins from the 1957 team. Edward Costley spoke for the 1969 team. My Panther football heroes are from the early 60's. Pete Burney, John Childers, David Fox and David Byrd are the guys who taught me how to win. I have seen a lot of Mart football. 99-yard runs from scrimmage twice. Exciting plays of past years, Billy Hyden running a kickoff back against Mexia, John Diaz's plays against Midway to win the first district game of the 1965 season. Roger Busby's perfect pass to Robert Jarrad on the first play of our game against Robinson to win the 1965 district championship. Gary Koester's block against a McGregor team. I was a freshman keeping stats and the player from McGregor slid all the way to the dressing room door at least 20 yards. And finally, there was Tony Baker's opening kickoff return against Groesbeck.

I will close with I was a privileged person to have played with the guys I played with. We won because the offensive line was National Honor Society. One person didn't make it because of conduct. When directions or plays were called, the line picked it up first time every time. Coach Burleson had leadership sayings on the wall, but the one that stuck with me was 'WINNING ISN'T EVERYTHING, IT IS THE ONLY THING,' by Coach Lombardi."

Jones' pronouncement of his love for Coach Burleson and their continuing to stay in contact 40 years after he played there is echoed by other players in other chapters of *Friday's Winners* about their respective coaches. Burleson also has great feelings about the players at Mart he coached during the 15-year span he headed the Panthers, 1964 to 1978. In the following interview, he discussed key games, the Mart tradition and even touched on the coming 2014 season. He began, "Mart had previously won one State Championship in 1957; however it was always in contention for the district championship and had been in the playoffs numerous times. Players were always competitive and the community thought of themselves as "Champions." The school administrators were very supportive of athletes, especially football as both the superintendent (Les Bryan) and the high school principal (Jim Kemp) had previously coached football at Mart High School. Both spent their entire educational career, which spread over 25 years each, at one school: Mart High School. There was an outstanding booster club that provided excellent support, but didn't interfere with the coaching staff."

Burleson got into talking about some key games with his appraisal of the biggest game he coached at Mart, "The most exciting was the State Championship game in 1969, we beat Sonora 28-0. Sonora had won state in 1968 and then came back to win it again in 1970 after Mart moved to AA. Our biggest district win was hard to say, but the game against Midway in 1965 led to the first district championship in several years. Mart won 13-6 which led to the district championship after going 5-5, 5-5 and 3-5-2 the previous three years." As far as the biggest playoff game other than the State Championship win over Sonora, Burleson stated, "It was the Quarter-Final game against White Oak in 1969. White Oak was undefeated and ranked #1 at the time. Mart won 12-7, scoring the winning TD with just a couple of minutes left in the game. The game was played under miserable conditions - about four inches of rain had fallen during the day - the water standing on the field had turned to mush. The temperature was 35 to 36 degrees with a light drizzle falling throughout the game. White Oak displayed outstanding sportsmanship following the game, extending their congratulations even though they were bitterly disappointed."

In talking about the most outstanding player(s) he coached at Mart, Burleson said, "During the 14 years I coached at Mart, there was a big amount of outstanding players. It would be unfair to single out just one. I couldn't start to name them all for fear I would leave out someone who was very special. The outstanding ones to me were those who had average ability, but wanted nothing more than to be a Mart Panther."

Burleson's coaching record at Mart for the years 1964 through 1978 was 96-46-8. The 1969 Class A State championship which Mart won with a 15-0 record represented his best year with the Panthers. For his entire coaching career which covered 24 years also at Desoto, Dawson and Red Oak, he had a record of 153 wins, 92 losses and 10 ties.

Though Burleson has been out of coaching now for over 30 years, he did offer an opinion about the 2014 version of the Panthers, "The anticipation is always the same at Mart-to play for the championship. Their strengths are the tradition and the outstanding coaching in the person of Rusty Nail and his staff, the administration, the parents and the kids."

In every one of these schools, there are people who aren't on the coaching staff or the administration who nevertheless contribute heavily to the success of the local programs in various ways. I mentioned Calvin Jones a few paragraphs earlier and the various ways he has stayed involved with the Panthers after graduating in 1971. There is another Mart graduate from the class of 1960 who specializes in keeping up with the Mart game records from the first year the Panthers played in 1912 until the present. Butch Walker never played any sports for Mart as he had to help his dad in his business after school and in the summer. Since 1998, he has built a web site that is very precise, very colorful and very informative on all the 1000+ games Mart has played in its history. The Mart website and the Longview website stand out to me as the best of the ones I go to for researching this book. In addition to being an outstanding historian and chronicler of Mart football, he is an avid Mart fan. In the words below, Walker touches on his passion and his role in keeping Mart citizens and fans informed about their beloved Panthers.

He begins, "I was born and raised in Mart. I have been a huge Mart Panther fan since I was old enough to understand the game. I didn't play sports in high school as I had to work for my dad. After I graduated in 1960, I joined the Air Force. I remained in the service for over 30 years, retiring in February 1991. I enrolled in college that year. When I graduated in 1995, I returned to Mart in January of 1996. Since then I have been to most of Mart's games, both at home and on the road.

The most memorable game that I watched the Panthers play was against Live Oak in a playoff game at Maverick Stadium at the University of Texas at Arlington in December 2000. It was a cloudy, overcast and windy day in the 40's. Both teams were undefeated. Mart had a 28-game win streak going. The game became a defensive struggle. The game turned in Live Oak's favor when the Buffaloes intercepted a Mart pass and returned it for a touchdown to grab a 7-0 lead late in the second quarter. It remained that way until very late in the fourth quarter. The Buffaloes were in possession of the ball and seemed to have the game in hand. But they failed to maintain control and the Panthers took over the ball with one and a half minutes left in the game. The Panthers worked their way downfield, keyed by a nice hook and ladder play that gave them a first down near the Buffalo 20. Another first down gave Mart a first and goal at the nine yard line. A pass to Rashi Sharp moved it to the two. Quan Cosby then bulled his way into the end zone to make it 7-6 with 39 seconds left in the game. Lyndell Strunck calmly booted the extra point for a 7-7 tie. The game went into overtime. Mart got the ball first. After three incomplete passes and facing fourth and 10 at the Live Oak 25, Quan tossed an arching ball to his twin brother, Quincy who caught it near the back of the end zone to give Mart a 13-7 lead. Strunck's kick was no good leaving Mart in a vulnerable position. But on Live Oak's first play, Rashi Sharp intercepted its pass and the game ended. Most of Live Oak's fans had already departed the stadium and were on their way to the parking lot when Mart's improbable comeback was mounted. They were dumbstruck when they realized Mart had won the game."

Walker described how he got into keeping Mart's records, "After I retired and returned to Mart, I began researching the history of Mart High School. I visited the Mart library and copied every game report from the inception of the program in 1912 to the current date. I began writing a column for the Mart paper that I call Panther Lore. I highlight the games that Mart has won over the years and include team stats, win-loss records and other information. I am beginning my sixteenth season of doing this with the start of the 2014 season."

The guy who was the difference maker in that Live Oak game Walker described as the most exciting was Quan Cosby. In that state championship year of 1999 and in 2000, he achieved a rare distinction of being named as five-time All-State player. Cosby went both ways as a starter which helped him be a five-time All-Stater. He was an All-State quarterback twice, defensive back twice and kick returner once. In 1999, he rushed for 1532 yards on 112 carries and scored 26 touchdowns. He passed for 1316 yards and 17 touchdowns. The next year, he ran for 1924 yards scoring 29 touchdowns and passed for 1405 yards and 13 touchdowns. He made seven touchdowns that year on five punt returns, one kickoff return and one interception. He also was an outstanding baseball player and as a senior was drafted into the California Angels organization. Of course, there were plenty of colleges wanting him to play football. He signed with Texas to play football, but deferred joining the Longhorns while he played four years of minor league ball. After Texas, he played in the NFL for several years, Indianapolis being his last stop as I mentioned to begin this chapter.

Cosby played on the varsity for four years from 1997 through 2000. His coach was Terry Cron all four years. The Panthers had a 51-6-0 record while Cosby played for Cron. He says of his coach, "Coach Cron is a Hall of Fame coach, one of the best ever, won state in three different classifications with three different teams. He reminds me of Phil Jackson. He had many talents, but sometimes the hardest thing on managing it is putting everyone in a position to succeed. He did exactly that and that was why he was able to win state and get there often." (Cron won the 1A state title at Bartlett in 1992, the 2A title at Mart in 1999 and the 3A title at Commerce in 2001. He coached for 22 years, winning 175 games, losing 94 games and tying three times. He began coaching at Round Rock and retired from coaching at Mansfield Timberview.)

Cosby picked up talking about the games that Mart played. "With the teams we had, district was interesting and most games were blowouts (In his final two years as a Panther, the team went 15-0-0 in 1999 outscoring their opponents 789 to 100 and 15-1-0 in 2000 outscoring their opponents 634 to 116). But my freshman year was probably the biggest game I was in. I was on defense and sacked Patrick Hudkta from Rogers five times. They were the number one team in the state and ended up making it all the way to the State Championship that year. It was a big game for our team and we started rolling after the significant win."

He spoke of Mart's playoff games, "It would have to be the State Championship game that we won because it was my most complete game I have ever played in my life, running and throwing and a kick return for a touchdown. I had a shoestring tackle on a punt return and an interception. It was kind of what we did, a video game type of deal that you only believe if you see the film."

Asked about his involvement with the current day Mart program, Cosby responded, "I will always talk to the Mart guys to continue the tradition of winning. I also have a cousin on the team (running back D'Marcus Cosby). I don't do as much, but there are many ex-players to talk to the kids and make it clear our ways and expectations."

The year after Quan last played was 2001. Tommy Roberson became the head coach. He coached at Mart for five seasons compiling a 40-19 record for that time. Three of his five teams went three deep in the playoffs, 9-4 in 2001, 11-2 in 2004 and 11-2 in 2005. In all, Roberson was in coaching for 31 years from 1977 through 2007. The other schools where he coached included Fairfield, West Rusk (New London), his alma mater - Grapeland, Moody, Buffalo, Groveton, Wortham, Dawson, Cleveland and Gatesville. He was a head coach for 16 of those 31 years running up a 107-68-0 record in those years.

Roberson commented about coaching in small communities in general, some key games he coached at Mart and concluded by naming the Mart players who stood out to him for their play. He begins, "The thing about coaching anywhere is the community traditions that you get to observe and be a part of during your time at each school. You can see the importance of those traditions by observing the faces in the crowd. At Mart, there is a certain level of expectation in the community that is felt by all involved with the football team. As a coach, if you don't live up to those expectations then you don't coach here very long. It is a double edge sword. It makes you better as a coach, but it can be a burden to your family. There's no doubt the fans will be there when the lights come on and they expect their children to perform at or above some level of other teams in school history. If they don't, then they are very vocal about their disappointment. Not just toward the coaches, but also to their own children."

"I suppose the most exciting win at Mart was not really a win at all. We were playing Alto in the third round of the playoffs in Palestine and the game did not go well for us until the last quarter. Then it was like our team transformed from mediocre to outstanding, mounting a comeback that ended up with us scoring the go ahead touchdown as time expired only to have it called back for a penalty that occurred about 40 yards away from any significant action. I could not have been more prouder of my team than I was that night. To come back and win and have it taken away and accept it with class shown was a testament to the team. In my heart, we won that game, but we just did not get to advance to the next round of the playoffs." (Alto won the game 27-22.)

The most important district game in my career at Mart must have been the double overtime victory over Buffalo. We did not play particularly well and Buffalo did. We put the game on Quincy Cosby's shoulders that night as he carried the ball 41 times and he doubled as a corner to shut down their best receiver. Too many big plays in that game to recall all of them, but trust me; it seemed like every time I turned around there was a crucial call to be made. That win allowed us to secure a playoff spot. Without it we would not have made the playoffs and I probably would not be writing this now. The most significant playoff victory was the same year as the Buffalo game We were the third place team and faced the #1 ranked Corrigan Camden Bulldogs in the first round.

Ironically it was also in Palestine. They were an awesome team that had many weapons. This was before the days of spread offenses and our greatest asset was to get the ball, keep it and score while running out the clock. We knew we had to score first and put up as many points as possible before they scored and try to force them to do things they did not like or do well. The coaches and the team could not have executed the game plan any better than we did that afternoon. We scored the first two touchdowns and converted two two-point conversions to take a 16-0 lead and never looked back. (The Panthers won 23-21.) I think the same can be said about this game as the Buffalo game. I felt my job was on the line. Mart had just won and played for state the previous two years and we were not expected to give Corrigan Camden much of a challenge. I have said many times that win saved my job."

Roberson discussed who some of the top players were at Mart. He began, "There were too many great offensive players to single out just one, but if I had to, it just might be Damian Davis. Extremely talented and gifted receiver. However I must mention a kid at Dawson, Jonathan Roberson. The most consistent receiver I ever coached. He was also our place kicker. He was also the coach's son. This meant he played under more pressure than anyone. And he performed under pressure very well. Coach's kids are readily more visible than any others. Their accomplishments and blemishes are magnified and there is no way to get around it. Fact of life.

It's easier to single out a defensive player. Colby Witt stands out not for just for play on the field, but also by being a student of the game. Colby was a linebacker on the 1999, 2000 and 2001 teams. Colby would take film home almost every week and study, breakdown and analyze opponents just like a coach. Several times he would come up on weekends and ask if we saw this or that about an opponent or a school. No wonder he went on to have an outstanding college career at McMurry and come back to Mart to help coach the 2010 state champion Mart Panthers."

Finally we come to the current head coach, Rusty Nail, who is preparing to coach his ninth Panther team. His eight years at their helm represents his entire head coaching experience. Not a bad record so far with 92 wins against 22 losses and two State Championships in that run. He credits the attraction of his coaching in Mart to "the tradition and support of all involved regardless of what role they have with the particular year's team."

When asked about games that stood out to him, Nail replied, "Probably the Semi-Final win over Canadian in 2010 in Abilene. They had pummeled us 38-7 in the State Championship game in 2008." He stated again that was the biggest game he's coached at Mart. There was only one district game that sticks in Nail's mind. He stated, "The only district game I remember is the one district game we have lost in my eight years here and that was Lovelady in 2009." To make things worse, Lovelady beat Mart at Mart 35-21 on October 16 that year. We previously heard what was said about the home record of the Panthers in the early 80s. A loss rarely happened because no self-respecting Panther player wanted to go into Read's Food Store on Saturday morning after a loss the night before and have an 80 year old grandmother call him out for not stopping their opponent.

Nail mentioned three players who have stood out to him as top players for Mart. On offense, he brought up Lee McClendon. "Lee McClendon was as accurate a passer as I have coached and was also an outstanding runner as well. The best all-around player in my tenure here is DeNerian Thomas, our current quarterback and linebacker. He will probably break all the records and overtake this role by season's end. Deshon Kinsey who is now a star linebacker at UMHB has been the best defensive player."

Nail might have been modest in assessing his team's prospects for 2014 as he answered, "If we stay healthy, we can compete with the best. Experience is a strength. Offense is a strength. Weakness will be changes and depth on defense. If we play great defense, we have a chance." Texas Football magazine in its new edition seems to think that Mart won't have any issues as they have them ranked #1 overall in Class 2A. Then they have the Panthers knocking off Refugio for the Division I State championship.

THE PLANO WILDCATS

FIRST YEAR THEY PLAYED: 1904
ALL TIME RECORD: 734-336-47
PERCENTAGE: 67.81%
PLAYOFF APPEARANCES: 48
STATE CHAMPIONSHIP GAMES WON: 1965, 1967, 1971, 1977, 1986, 1987, 1994
STATE CHAMPIONSHIP GAMES LOST: 1978, 1993

If there's any one team in my list that has transformed itself the most, it's the Plano Wildcats. Much of that transformation has come about because of the changes that have come about as Plano has grown from a very small farming community of 500 shortly after its founding in 1873 to a small town of 3695 citizens by 1960 and from that point on exploded its population on a decade by decade basis to today's 274, 409 people. Plano Senior High has seen its athletic programs also explode as the student body mushroomed in size. The Wildcats have captured seven State Championships beginning at the 2A level in 1965 and 1967. In 1971, they added a 3A title to their trophy case. Six years later, they picked up the 4A state championship. Then in three other years, they added the 5A title to their growing collection of metal. That was in 1986, 1987 and 1994. That '87 version of the Wildcats was voted the #2 team in the United States in the final poll by USA Today, finishing behind North Hills of Pittsburgh, Pennsylvania. Now as the 2014 season nears, the Wildcats have been realigned to the new Class 6A which gives them the opportunity to win state at this new level and further extend a record of winning at all these different class levels. That record as it now stands will never be broken. Adding a 6A title would be an achievement that would put Plano in a category where almost no team could ever catch it. Of the schools in *Friday's Winners,* only Mart could achieve state titles in all classes if for some reason, something happened to its economy to dramatically increase its population in the same manner that has happened in Plano. And of course, if the Panthers continued their winning tradition.

It's pretty rare for a coach to spend his entire coaching career in one school district, let alone all the rest of his career as an educator moving into administrative jobs after he is through coaching. Tom Kimbrough is one of the rarities, still on the job with the Plano ISD 47 years after he first went to work for it. His first 23 years in Plano was in coaching and teaching. He became the head coach of the Wildcats in 1976 taking over for John Clark who had continued the Plano legacy with two State Championships in a career that spanned 10 years, 1966 through 1975 and generated a 107-17-0 record. Kimbrough held the head coaching position from 1976 through 1991. He led the Wildcats to a 171-28-7 record and the three State Championships in 1977, 1986 and 1987. Here below are his comments on his career, "This marks my 47th year in the Plano ISD. All of my coaching days,1968 to 1991, were spent at Plano Senior High. Having been employed by only one school in my career makes it unique. Seeing Plano grow from a small district to a large district while it is achieving success from both an athletic and an academic standpoint makes it special to me and my family."

He discussed the games he coached, "There were many exciting wins. All the State Champion games were exciting. In addition to them, the games with Permian, Highland Park and Temple and a number of others stand out."

(Just to list those games that took place in the playoffs with those schools he mentioned and others in *Friday's Winners* takes up a good quarter page. Some of them are mentioned elsewhere, but here is a list of those games. In 1977: the 29-28 Quarter-Final win over Highland Park, the 3-0 Semi-Final win over Permian. 1978: the 13-13 Bi-District win over Tyler based on first downs, the 15-14 Regional win over Temple, the 6-3 Semi-Final win over Permian. 1979: the 19-16 Regional loss to Temple. 1980: the 23-7 Bi-District win over Longview, the 16-0 Regional win over Temple, the 23-21 Regional loss to Highland Park. 1983: the 20-14 Regional win over Temple. 1984: the 17-7 Area loss to Highland Park and 1987: the 29-21 Semi Final win over Permian.)

Kimbrough continued talking about some of the players he coached on the Wildcats, "The defensive players that stood out were Billy Ray Smith and Pat Thomas. Billy Ray played for us in 1977 and 1978. Both years we played in the State Championship game. He went on to success at Arkansas and with San Diego in the NFL. Thomas who went on to A & M and LA in the NFL matched Billy Ray's success played while I was an assistant in 1970-1972. Offensively we were blessed with many talented players. Rex Burkhead, who went on to Nebraska, would certainly be among the top. He didn't play while I was coaching." Burkhead rushed for 1858 yards on 306 carries and 29 touchdowns in 2007. In 2008, he rushed for 1762 yards on 255 carries scoring 28 more touchdowns.

Obviously, the ever increasing enrollment at Plano Senior coupled with the ever increasing growth of the City of Plano's population meant that there wouldn't be enough seating capacity in the stadium for the Wildcats home games if the school district didn't provide for new stadiums as the growth continued. Smitty Minton who was in charge of stadium facilities for 25 years for the district told me about the progression of stadiums from the beginning in 1904 when the players would go to a vacant lot with rakes and hoes to clear the weeds and trash about two hours ahead of game time. I also read the information compiled by super Plano fan Bart Benne who wrote the book about the first 85 years of Plano football titled, *The Best High School Football in the Country*. Smitty told me the first field was called Rice Field. Bart wrote of a facility called the Oil Mill Field that preceded it. Rice Field was named by the school board in 1925. I was reminded of the Hondo Field when I read that the south end of Rice Field was lower than the north and that players sometimes suffered injuries because the fans were allowed to be too close to the field. In both cases, there were adjustments made to resolve these issues. The seating capacity at Rice Field was 2,000 fans.

According to Smitty, the next field was Williams Field which opened in 1964. There was seating for 8,000 fans in it. The next stadium started a new tradition in Plano when it was named for former coach John Clark. He was the athletic director when the field was named for him and opened in 1977. It had seating for slightly over 14,000 fans. In 1979, Richardson beat Plano 3-0 in a game played there on October 12th. The victorious Richardson students attempted to burn their school initials into the artificial turf at Clark Field some time after the game. Their act created enough damage to the field so that the remaining two of the home games that season were played at Texas Stadium.

Texas Stadium became the scene of a number of playoff games for Plano. According to Benne, the Wildcats had played 24 games there through the time he had recorded data, the 1989 season. Their record was 18-5-1. It was said that Plano won more games on the Dallas Cowboys home field than the Cowboys did during the two state championship seasons.

Smitty Minton was recognized in a 2007 Plano High School Hall of Fame ceremony possibly for two different reasons. The first would be for his 25 years of service to the district taking care of the stadium facilities and preparing them for the games to be played on them. Or possibly, it is because he might well be the Wildcats' #1 fan. He moved to Plano in 1954 and attended all of the home games and some of the away games for the next six years. Then he became a fan in earnest. Since the 1960 season, he has missed only three games total, at home or on the road. The first miss came when the Wildcats played Brownwood in the 1971 state Semi-Final game at Amon Carter Field in Fort Worth. He had flown to Houston on business as he worked for the Borden Company then. As he said, "If I could have had the plane land in Meachem Field in Fort Worth, I probably could have made it. But of course it landed at Love Field and I just had my wife go to the game without me." In 2013, he suffered a mini stroke which grounded him for two games. So in 54 years, he has seen right at 600 Plano games and missed only three games. That is team loyalty personified.

There is one more stadium in the Plano ISD real estate holdings. In 2004, Kimbrough Stadium was built to help accommodate all the games the district played. Like its predecessor stadium, Clark Field, it was named for the athletic director at that time, former head coach Tom Kimbrough. It has seating capacity for 9800 fans.

Smitty Minton isn't the only passionate Plano fan by any means. There are a group of fans who call themselves the Committee who have gathered virtually every Thursday night since the 1986 State Championship to drink beer, eat pizza and discuss Wildcat football. There are about 25 to 30 men who spasmodically attend these gatherings, sometimes dipping in attendance to less than 10, but nevertheless getting together because they care about Plano football. There are those who have written odes and poems dedicated to the Wildcats. An example of each is carried below with the permission of Roger Toney, another passionate Wildcat fan, who has put a lot of written material together about Plano. The poem was written by Edwina Patterson, a Plano Wildcat's mother. Her son is Russell Patterson from the class of 1987. Her poem is appropriately called *A Football Player's Mother.*

The Plano Wildcats

A Football Player's Mother
You know, it takes someone special
To be a football player's mother
She really is a breed
Like unto no other.
From the very beginning it seems,
That something sets her apart
I really think it's because
God gave her an extra big heart.
He knew it would take someone unique
To care for that little boy.
And as he grew and was nurtured
Would bring her infinite joy!
She'd need to know how to cook everything
From Belgium waffles to scrambled eggs.
She'd need to know how to clean, especially
Those grass stains in blue jean legs.
She must have knowledge of medicine,
Hospitals, aspirin and bandaids;
And perform ten tasks at once
As if she had several maids.
She must definitely have a sense of humor,
And be able to laugh at life
As she sits in the stands having
to deal with all that tension and strife!
She must know terms such as
Shotgun, blitz, flex and safety,
And not cry out when
someone squashes her baby!
And when that son is disappointed,
Hurt, discouraged, or blue,
She must reach deep down inside her
And know exactly what to do,
ABOVE ALL ELSE......and time....
And time again,
She must be able to show

How very much she loves him!
So you see, it does take someone special
To be a football player's Mother
Just look at my Mom–
You need look no further!

The ode is titled *To a Plano Wildcat*. The author for it is anonymous. It started appearing about 1989 as a handout to the fans.

To A Plano Wildcat
There are little eyes upon you,
And they are watching night and day;
There are little ears that quickly
Take in every word you say;
There are little hands all eager
To do everything you do;
And a little boy who's dreaming
Of the day he'll be a Wildcat-just like you!
You're the little guy's idol,
You're the wisest of the wise,
In his little mind about you,
No suspicions ever rise.
He believes in you devoutly,
Vows that all you say and do,
He'll do and say the same thing
When he becomes a Wildcat-just like you!
Now this starry-eyed little fellow,
Thinks you do everything just right,
And his heart is always pounding
As he watches you on Friday night;
You are setting an example
Your life is put to the test it's true-
By the little boy who's longing
To be a Plano Wildcat-just like you!

Gerald Brence is now the athletic director of the Plano ISD as well as the author of two books, The 70-30 Split *and* Ox in the Culvert. The first is, as the continuation of the title says, a practical guide to motivation, leadership and coaching. The second is Brence's first novel ever, a historical tale of the Old West in early day Texas and the California gold rush era. But before Brence moved into the administrative offices of the Plano ISD and also began to pen how to books and novels, he spent 16 years as the head coach of the Wildcats from 1992 through 2007. He built a record of 120-70-11 during which time, Plano soared to the top of Texas high school footballdom as the 1994 State Champions and dropped all the way down to the bottom of the barrel of Texas high school footballdom with an 0-10-0 record in 2003 and then came back all the way to a Semi-Final appearance, a 30-27 overtime loss to Euless Trinity in his final season of 2007.

His first year to be head coach after coming up from the assistant coaching ranks was 1992. He began as an assistant coach at Vines High School, part of the Plano ISD in 1981 and 1982. Then he became an assistant at Plano Senior High from 1983 through 1991 before his promotion to head football coach of the Wildcats in 1992. His first team reached the Regional game. The next year, Plano went all the way to the State Championship game losing to Converse Judson 36-13. In his third year, Brence led the Wildcats all the way to the State Championship beating Katy decisively 28-7. The next two years saw Plano's season end at the Bi-District game level. The Wildcats missed the playoffs in 1997, but got all the way to the Quarter-Finals the next year. It was back to the Bi-District level in '99. In 2000, the Wildcats had one of those When Paths Crossed moments playing a playoff game against another team in Friday's Winners in the Area round. Tyler got by the Wildcats 21-15 that year. But Plano made it back to the Area game in 2001. Then came the three year drought of losing seasons of 3-7-0, 0-10-0 and 4-6-0 before Plano righted the ship again. Brence took Plano to the Quarter-Finals in 2005 and then to the Semi-Finals as mentioned above in his final season of 2007.

Brence commented about his coaching days beginning by saying, "The family grew up in the field house." The 1994 State Championship game is his most exciting win at Plano. He considers the biggest district game he was involved in to be the 1985 game between Plano and Plano East which was won by Plano East. Brence mentions two games as the two biggest playoff games during his head coaching reign, the 2005 Southlake Carroll game and the 2007 Trinity Semi-Final loss in overtime.

As for top players that he coached on the Wildcats, he stated that Scooter Asel, the quarterback on the 1994 team stood out on offense and he cited three players on defense, all from different years for the Wildcats. There was Mike Nelson from the '93 team, Judd Smith from the '95 team and David Hall from the '96 team. Asel did an interview which will follow next in the chapter.

Robert "Scooter" Ansel was on the Wildcat varsity for two years, 1993 and 1994. In his first year, Scooter played cornerback, wide receiver and free safety. As Brence mentioned above, he stood out as a quarterback on the '94 State Champion team, but he also played wide receiver and free safety. For honors, he was selected second team All-District cornerback in 1993. In 1994, he was the co MVP of the State Championship game and the starting quarterback at the Coaches McDonald's All Star game. He received a scholarship to play football for Eastern Kentucky University which he did from 1995 through 1999.

He had a lot to say about the Plano experience, "At the time there were two schools in Plano, Plano and Plano East. We all grew up together playing against each other since we were seven years old. Then you split up and in middle school and start your allegiance to one of the senior highs. For me it was prior to that because my older brother Richard played on the '86 and '87 Plano State Champs. I was a nine and 10 year old rug rat running around at practice and the games. Playing for Plano was all I wanted to do growing up. Seniors made up about 90% of the team. Plano is a two year high school and at that time, a freshman and sophomore could not play on the team. If you were a junior and made the team, that was big time. There were only 12 to 15 of us that made it that year, which was typical. I can still remember calling my brother and telling him. He said, 'Congrats, now go get two state rings like I have.' I got one and he still holds it over my head."

I asked him about his coach and he replied, " Gerald Brence was very enthusiastic! Plano was about discipline and accountability. You had to do your job or you would be out. We had guys on the second team OL that didn't play their junior years and then went on to start at major Division I college programs. The competition was very high. Coach Brence was great to me. The coaching staff was extremely dedicated, working into the night almost every day of the week. I think this was the norm that was set by Coach Kimbrough. It was always Faith, Family, Football. I can remember that saying all the way down to seventh grade football and the coaches in middle school. He was the kind of guy that you never wanted to disappoint both on and off the field. I have a lot of respect for him and what he did for me."

Asel continued on about the Plano program, "The way that the coaches planned the program was great. Started in 7th grade all the way through the 12th grade. We just kept adding new wrinkles each year and when we got to Plano in our senior year, we were a machine. I think Coach Clark probably set that standard and Coach Kimbrough and Brence followed suit and perfected it."

Asked about his actual playing experience, he replied, "I had never played QB in my life. My junior year, Jason Little started at QB and in the last game of the year, Coach Brence moved Mike Nelson over to QB from FS. Plano/Plano East game. Nelson breaks a 50+ yard touchdown to give us the win. We go to the playoffs and he is the QB. I move from CB to FS. We go to state and lose that year. In the spring, Brence calls me in and says he is going to have me taking snaps with the second team offense during spring practice. Jason Little is again on tap to be the starter. Nelson graduated and went on to play football at Northwestern."

He added more about his playing status as a Wildcat, "So starting FS and 2nd team QB. I have no thoughts on the matter, just whatever the team needs. Senior year, third game of the year, I tackle a running back for Mesquite and get a concussion. It knocked me out of the next game. The Saturday/Sunday after game four, Brence calls me in his office and says, 'If things are going well against Richardson this week, I am going to move you to QB in the second or third series, so be ready.'

Asel continued, "All week at practice, I was no contact because of the concussion. I just practiced in a helmet and our gray workout clothes. Friday rolls around and sure enough 2nd or 3rd series I go in. You can ask any of the guys in the huddle at that time. I walked in the huddle and said I was going to take them to the Promised Land. I know it sounds corny, but few of us have talked about me saying that 15-20 years after that huddle. First play option keeper gets about 8-10 yards. I ended the game with a little over 100 yards rushing and more importantly we won."

He talked about the end of the regular season and the playoffs, " So fast forward to game 9 and 10 of the season…….Lake Highlands and Plano East. Going into those games, we were already in the playoffs. 1994, each district has three teams in the playoffs. Highest enrollment goes to Division I playoff and the other two go to Division II. We proceed to get rolled by both teams. They just whipped our butts up and down the field. We ended up third in district, but since we had the highest enrollment, we went to the Division I playoff bracket. We got into the playoffs and just got on a roll. It's hard to believe that we lost the last two games of the year and then went 5-0 in the playoffs to win the State Championship. One of the most special games in the five game run was a 10-0 State Semi-Final defeat of Odessa Permian at Ratliff Stadium. They hadn't been scored on the entire playoffs. We scored on a classic Plano play. 28 Tight End was the play. It was a designed QB keeper around the left end about 35 yards out. I think Odessa's offense crossed the 50 maybe three or four times. I know they didn't get inside our 20 yard line. Unbelievable team effort."

He continued, "I can remember one time in the fourth quarter looking up at the crowd on the home side and it was silent and everyone was sitting down. That is when I knew we were going to State. To make it even sweeter, the last time Odessa played Plano was in 1987 in the State Semi-Finals, my brother's senior year and Plano won that one as well."

Asked about his current association with the Plano program, Asel said, "We don't do much. I like to bring my kids around Plano as much as I can, but we don't live in Plano and I am trying to get them to gravitate towards the high school that they will be going to. I still go to a game every once in a while. I will also swing by practice from time to time to see the coaches and speak to the players if they want me to. There is a lot of history with me and my brother six years apart with three state championship rings and a runner up ring. There were a couple of us on the team like that. Kind of interesting."

Scooter has stayed connected with football as an official in the Big 12, Mountain West and *Southland Conferences.* His regular day job is with Northwestern Mutual Insurance in the Park Cities area of Dallas.

Asel might have been chosen co-MVP of the State Champion game which Plano won over Katy 28-7 at Kyle Field, but there were two other heroes and perhaps MVPs for the Wildcats for what they did in the fourth quarter. What might come to mind for fourth quarter heroics is making a drive-stopping interception or throwing the game winning touchdown pass into the end zone as the clock ran out; or running for the touchdown or making the game saving tackle. It all depends on what the situation is. But for the Wildcats, its two heroes are recognized for what they did in the locker room at Kyle Field before the game was over. Chris Cason and Nathan Hale caught two thieves rifling the pockets of their teammates' clothes.

Brence tells about the experience in his book, *The 70-30 Split.* He wrote, "We started the fourth quarter with a 28-0 lead. All of a sudden, two of our reserve players, (Cason and Hale) came up to me and said, 'Coach, we have to go to the bathroom.' I was a little perturbed, but I let them go. What happened next became Texas High School football history. The two players walked into the locker room and found two crooks going through our players' belongings. As soon as they saw our players, the crooks bolted for the door. The two football players chased them right out the door and onto the street outside the stadium."

He continued, "You have to understand that the press box was on the other side of the stadium from our locker room. Everybody up there watched two football players in full pads chasing two crooks on foot. The players caught them and pounced on them. Then they realized they had to get back to the game. I had no idea any of this was happening. We won the game and the media was all over me. My wife ran over to me, and I gave her one of those token hugs you give someone when you are really busy. That was the dumbest thing I did all day. That put me in the dog house for a month. All the TV people wanted to know about was the chase. I didn't even know what they were talking about. Late that night we were back in Plano watching the news. The big story was about two football players chasing down crooks at the State Championship game. Nobody ever said anything about Plano putting names on the back of their jerseys."

Brence's son, Collin Brence, played for the Wildcats varsity from 2008 through 2010. He was a fullback and a strong safety (rover). Twice in his three years on the team, the Wildcats reached the second round of the playoffs and to the first round once. He earned some honors for his play all three years. He was All-District Honorable Mention Fullback as a sophomore. As a junior, he was a second team All-District defensive back. As a senior, he was a unanimous first team All-District defensive back, first team All Collin County defensive back, Associated Press 5A first team All-State defensive back and THSCA first team Academic All-State.

Collin described the special experience that is being a part of the Plano program, "Plano Senior High has a history and following like none other. Everyone in town pays attention to what happens on those Friday nights and John Clark Stadium is almost always full. The crowd is electric and consistent whether the team is winning or losing. Playing for Plano made it impossible for me to play anything other than big-time college football. I wanted to play in front of bigger and better crowds. Coming from Plano narrowed my choices way down."

He said of his Plano coach, "Coach Jaydon McCullough is about as passionate as a man can get. He loves the game and loves his players and coaches even more. You wanted to win for him, and he wanted us to be successful. I will always be able to call Coach McCullough family."

I asked him about significant games for him in his Plano career. He responded, "My favorite game I ever played as a Wildcat was against our crosstown rival, Plano East in 2010 as a senior. We both came into the game needing to win in order to stay in the playoff hunt, and both teams were on a hot streak. Neither team liked each other at all. Ultimately we played possibly the most dominant game ever of the series winning 38-0. We always want to beat East by a big margin, but to hold them to a shutout was unbelievable. I had a bunch of tackles in the game and two forced fumbles, including my only blitz and sack in high school."

About playoff games, Collin said, "I always loved playing against Euless Trinity. We never beat them out of the three years we played them, but you could always count on an amazing game. I always respected their program and loved defending their offense. Another game I will always remember is when we played Duncanville in the first round of 2009. We were down by 21 points in the second half and came back to win. The team really came together and rallied to win one of the best come –from-behind games in Plano history."

He closed with, "Those who get to play for the Plano Wildcats and wear the maroon and white are extremely special. There have been countless players that came before them and laid it on the line to carry on the winning tradition. The Plano fans are extraordinary and have always been the best out there. It is an honor to step out onto John Clark Field and play in front of them. Those

Friday nights are truly some of my favorite memories. Never take them for granted, because you will miss them someday."

Collin mentioned above about his desire to play only big time college football. He was true to his word. He had offers to play at University of Louisana-Monroe, Columbia and Holy Cross. He decided to walk on at Baylor University. He remained a walk on at Baylor until the 2014 season when he was awarded a scholarship and became a starter for the Bears.

Collin also mentioned his love and feel of a family connection for his Plano coach, Jaydon McCullough. It's no wonder as McCullough is Plano personified. He played for the Wildcats under Tom Kimbrough in 1979 and 1980. After he graduated from Plano, he studied at Dallas Baptist University earning a Bachelors of Science degree in 1985. Then he went into coaching, perhaps with the goal of getting back to Plano High as a coach as soon as possible. After stints in the Allen ISD and the Pleasant Grove ISD, he joined the Plano coaching staff in 1994, just in time to be a part of a State Championship team. He was the defensive coordinator. In 2008, he replaced Gerald Brence as the head coach of the Wildcats. Brence became the PISD athletic director.

Since then, McCullough has gotten the Wildcats to the second round of the playoffs twice and to the first round three times in his six years at the helm. His first year in 2008 has been his most productive as the Wildcats went 10-2. Then it has been 5-7 in 2009, 7-4 in 2010, 4-6 in 2011, 5-6 in 2012 and 7-4 in 2013. That's a record of 38-29-0 so far. He was working very hard to prepare the Wildcats for a better season in 2014. His passion for his team and the task ahead of them came out in a talk I had with him in early August, 2014. A product of the Plano system and a participant as a player and a coach in its successful traditions, McCullough is in a position to get Plano its first ever 6A State Championship should the Wildcats do well for him. That would be another notch in the gun belt of the third most winning high school team of Texas and put him in the record books along with the other Plano coaches who have helped the Wildcats create their big successes.

THE TEMPLE WILDCATS

FIRST YEAR THEY PLAYED: 1905
ALL-TIME RECORD THROUGH 2013: 710-340-52
PERCENTAGE: 66.78%
PLAYOFF APPEARANCES: 40
STATE CHAMPIONSHIP GAMES WON: 1979, 1992
STATE CHAMPIONSHIP GAMES LOST: 1940, 1941, 1951, 1952, 1976

Like the trains that have chugged through the major rail center that is the town of Temple for over 100 years, the Wildcats of Temple High have also chugged along for over a century building a trail of victories, making them fourth on the list of the most wins among Texas high school football teams. Despite bumps along the way, the Wildcats gathered enough steam during the 28-year tenure of Bob McQueen as the head coach to get two State Championships and, for a while, the title as king of the hill leading all Texas high schools in total football victories.

One of the first bumps was the suspension from the UIL from competition with other UIL schools for the entire 1939 season. That came about because of the team coaches being found guilty of illegal recruiting before the season. So the Wildcats played against junior college teams and had a 9-1 record against the older players. Perhaps being forced to play older teams because of the illegal recruiting helped build the team for the next two seasons as Temple played for the State Championship both years. But they lost to Amarillo in 1940 by a 20-7 margin and to Wichita Falls 13-0 for the 1941 State Championship. A decade later, they again made it to the 3A State Championship games for 1951 and 1952, but got unseated each time by the Breckenridge Buckaroos, 20-14 in '51 and 28-20 in '52.

One of the best things that happened to Temple during those first two tries at the State Championship was the emergence of Keifer Marshall as a starter for the Wildcats. He went both ways for Coach Les (Fats) Cranfill, as the center on offense and as a linebacker on defense. Against Dallas in a 1940 game, he intercepted a pass and returned it 70 yards for a touchdown. He talked about the 1942 season, "After losing at state again in 1941, our coach scheduled us to play the top teams throughout Texas. We beat Austin High (7-0), Corsicana (20-7) and Lubbock (13-6), but lost to Waco (7-0) and Amarillo. We rode the train to Amarillo for that game. It had rained so hard up there that the Amarillo officials postponed our scheduled Friday night game until Saturday night. That helped Amarillo to have the field dry out a little. The Sandies beat us 13-0." Temple didn't make the playoffs that year. Marshall graduated in 1943 and went to Texas to play on a football scholarship. He joined the Marine Corps the next year and was sent to the Pacific where some of the heaviest fighting occurred. His company of 252 Marines went to Iwo Jima where they got surrounded by Japanese soldiers and fought in a battle that lasted over 36 hours. His company received no reinforcements or additional supplies during that period. Only Marshall and five other Marines in that company of 252 men survived the battle.

After the war, he returned to Texas and finished playing football and found his bride to be, Tammy. They have been married 66 years and live in Temple where he has served as mayor. He continues to run his insurance agency today and participate in civic activities. I was in his office on August 1, 2014, to meet him in person for the first time. He was in a suit and tie for a normal business day, very congenial and eager to talk about Temple football. There were two items in his office that were attention grabbing and reflected what had happened in his life. One was a yellow brick on the corner of his deck. On it was printed his name, Keifer Marshall, Jr., his affiliation, Temple Wildcat and his years on the team, 1940-1942. He told me that it had come from the old locker room when they redid the stadium. The other item is a pencil drawing hanging on a wall to his right of the six Marines raising the flag at Iwo Jima, one of the most beloved symbols of the American spirit. Being in a room looking at that symbol of courage and sacrifice with a man who had actually survived Iwo Jima was a moment I had never experienced. It meant a lot to me to have a chance to meet such an American hero while trying to uncover his life as a Temple Wildcat. Keifer is also covered in my chapter, Football, a Family Tradition, as he is the first generation of three generations of his family who played for Temple High.

I asked Bob McQueen to contribute his comments about his coaching career at Temple which he graciously agreed to do. He has been retired since the 1998 season and tries to get in as much time as possible fishing with his sons Mark and Scott as well as with friends. Still, he found the time to write a letter that covered his 28 years coaching Temple in great detail and touched on his first four years as a head coach at Mexia. Below is his letter, one that will bring back many memories for Wildcat fans of those days of success fueled by the passion through which he led the Wildcats to their greatest successes on the gridiron.

"My name is Bob McQueen. I have been retired for 14 years. I coached for Hayden Fry at SMU. My first and only other head coaching job was at Mexia High where I worked for four years. We had some of the greatest young people that I've had the privilege of working with. We won the district championship three of the four years we were there. After Mexia, I joined Coach Fry's staff. From SMU I had the opportunity to become the head coach at my alma mater. I played high school football at Temple High and since I was a ninth grader, I wanted to be a coach and my dream was to be the head coach at Temple High School to bring Temple its first State Championship. It was my good fortune to serve as Head Football Coach and Athletic Director at Temple High School for 28 years. During that time we were able to win two State Championships in the top classification in Texas. In 1979 we were 4A champs, 15-0. At that time, 4A was the top classification and only one team out of each district went to the playoffs. When we won the championship in 1992 (15-1), two teams out of each district went to the playoffs and there was a 5A Division I (large) and a 5A Division II (small). We won 5A Division II and Converse Judson won 5A Division I. Bill Farney, AD of the UIL and a friend told me he thought the 1992 Wildcat team might have been the best team he had ever seen. Judson was a mega school and during that season we were fortunate enough to defeat them at their place 37-21 in a non-district game. It was the first time they had lost at home in over 10 years. That season, we also defeated the previous year's state champs, Odessa Permian (20-14), in a non-district game." Temple recovered a fumble late in the fourth quarter to preserve that lead.

"In Temple, we have always had great fan support. We always felt like they were a factor in our success. Some of our opponents would try to schedule our game on Thursday nights to cut down on our crowd. We had many wonderful friends and supporters, but the greatest thing about coaching in Temple is the young people you are privileged to work with. I saw my first Wildcat football game when I was in the fourth grade. My teacher had a brother who was the starting center for the Wildcats and my mom's second cousin was a Wildcat star. Many years later, I was fortunate enough to hire him to work with us on our staff.

From the fourth grade on I was a Wildcat whether I was playing football with my friends on the playground at school, or at the vacant lot next door, in junior high, or the B-Team in high school or finally on the varsity when I was a junior. That's the way we are in Temple. We grow up wanting to be a Wildcat. Our heroes are the dads, uncles, cousins, even granddads who played before us. Kids grow up wanting to wear a certain jersey number because it was the number of their hero. We had great assistant coaches and they worked hard at teaching kids great football, but also great lifetime skills. We wanted our kids to be tough and disciplined, but we also wanted them to be humble gentlemen off the field.

Temple kids love their coaches and will try to model after them. They, like our assistant coaches, were the hardest working kids I've ever been around. One of the greatest compliments our kids ever received was when the head coach of our biggest rival was leaving his post to take another job. He asked me out for lunch at which time he asked me two questions. One, he wanted to know about the defense we were running and he wanted to know what we did to make our kids so tough. I talked to him a little about our defense and to his second question, that's just the way our kids are. They are tough and physical. That's what we expected of them. Another compliment was made by another rival, dear friend and one of the better coaches in the state. Late in the game on fourth and nine, one of their defensive players slung our quarterback by the jersey in a complete circle and he stayed on his feet and completed the pass for a first down on the game winning drive. We nearly scored too soon because we won the game with an interception in the end zone in the closing seconds of the game. After the game, a reporter asked him what happened. His response, 'They are Temple and they just do things like that.'

Over the years, I have been privileged to coach in many very exciting games. And in looking back all the way to high school and college as a player and in my 39 years as a coach, nearly every year we had a game we won just because we tried harder, worked harder or were tougher. We always wanted to be heavy in the intangibles. Probably the most exciting game I coached in Temple was in 1975 in a district game against Bryan High School. This was the eighth game of the season and they were ranked as the #1 high school football team in America. In order to accommodate the crowd, they moved the game to Kyle Field on the Texas A & M campus. The game was played before approximately 22.000 fans. They had three or four players who went on to play in the NFL. Their star back was Curtis Dickey. At half time our players had played their hearts out, but Dickey had broken three long runs and they were ahead 21-6. When we went into the dressing room, I called the kids together and on the chalkboard I wrote:

> 21-6 (halftime score)
> +12 (2 TD's)
> +4 (2-2pt plays)
> 21-22 (Wildcats win)

Lester Ward, one of the best defensive players we ever had, broke his foot on the last play of the first half. He hobbled up to the chalk board and wrote, "Faith in one another."

We kicked off to them to start the second half and finally stopped them when our great safety, Larry Flowers (Texas Tech, New York Giants) hit Dickey after he caught a screen pass and knocked him out of both shoes. From there, we drove the length of the field running "49 Sweep" nine consecutive times with Flowers carrying the ball each time. We scored and went for two and made it. Late in the game, our great QB Mark Jermstad hit Flowers for a TD on a post route off of a play action. We went for two and our little tailback, Charles Young, outran Curtis Dickey to the corner of the end zone....22-21. Interesting sidebar. Dickey won state in the 100 meter and Charles Young ran the lead off leg on the 4x100 meter relay team at the University of Houston that set the world record in that event. The anchor leg was a kid by the name of Carl Lewis. That Wildcat team taught us how to win the big game. After the game, Billy Packard of A & M gave us the chalkboard. We had it glazed and framed and it hung in the Wildcat dressing room from 1975 to 2012 as a reminder to our kids to never give up.

Over the 28 years I coached in Temple, we have been a part of many great games. Over the years, Temple had been to the State Championship game several times, but had never been able to win the title. We actually played for the championship in 1976 and lost to San Antonio Churchill (10-0). They were good and we had two of our best players injured. They were a big school and our enrollment was always between 2100-2300 in the top four grades. For example, we got to play Plano in the playoffs and they had around 6000 in their top four grades. We were always one of the smaller schools in our UIL classification. In 1979, we beat Plano (19-16 in Regional) on the way to winning the State Championship which we won against Spring Branch Memorial (28-6). Plano was probably the most talented team we played that year in the playoffs. That was the most driven team and coaching staff I've ever been around. The year before we were stopped in a one point loss to Plano at Texas Stadium (15-14 in Regional). Our 1979 team was determined that it wouldn't happen to them. They were on a mission and they finished 15-0 State Champions.

In 1992 we beat Houston Yates 38-20 for the state title. It was a close game until our great defensive back, Derrick Bates, hit their star receiver on a pass play in front of their bench. His helmet, the ball and his chin strap and mouth piece went in different directions. They looked like the Dallas Cowboys, but they couldn't stop our little back, Delarius Wilson and Gerald Watson on the zones and counter and our great QB, Adrian Woodson who made great plays running and passing. That year in the Semi-Final game, we played Larry Dipple and his Amarillo Sandies. They were extremely well coached, but we probably had a little more talent than them. We met them at Wichita Falls and it was a great game, but we were fortunate enough to come out on top. (38-7)

Over the years we have been fortunate to coach many great players and even more great human beings. If I had to pick one offensive player, it would have to be Kenneth Davis who later made All-American at TCU and played for the Buffalo Bills. Kenneth was not only a great talent, but he was about as competitive on game day as anyone I've coached. There were so may others but I hesitate to mention them because I might leave one out (Like Russell Mikeska, A & M, Atlanta Falcons. At Mexia, I coached Ray Rhodes who has five or six Super Bowl rings, played for the New York Giants and was Head Coach of the Philadelphia Eagles. Certainly the best all-around player I ever coached. Very tough and a great person with a great Mom and Dad.

Defensively I don't know where to start. Lester Ward (phenomenal athlete and super tough) played for Baylor, Derrick Bates (BYU) at safety. Ypres Thomas was our Sam linebacker in '92 (All-American at Texas State). Rose Conde was a great linebacker. Chris Wilson was an unblockable nose guard. There are so many of the kids we coached that were just great high school football players. They didn't meet the college criteria, but they gave you everything they had every day in practice and more than they had on game day. That's why it was such an honor to coach them and be a part of their lives for a little while."

McQueen coached at Temple from 1972 until he retired after the 1999 season. His record with the Wildcats was 242 wins, 78 losses and seven ties. For his entire career which also encompassed the four years at Mexia, he had 276 wins, 86 losses and nine ties.

One of the first players on his 1972 team was David President. A junior that year, he played tight end. He added free safety and kicker to his positions in 1973, his senior year. He made All-District on both sides of the ball that season as well as All-Central Texas at tight end. His junior year, he was second team All-District tight end. He got a scholarship to Southwest Texas State (now Texas State) as a tight end. If his name is sounding familiar to you, it might be because he is the first generation Wildcat team member listed in the chapter, Football, a Family Tradition. Or it might be because his grandson, Chad President, the third generation in that family to be a Wildcat, is drawing rave reviews as the starting quarterback for the 2014 Temple team and is well enough thought of for his quarterback skills that Art Briles has gotten a commitment from him to play the QB position at Baylor after graduation.

David and I sat down on August 1, 2014 to talk about Temple football and his time playing for McQueen in his first two seasons 42 years ago. David commented, "That winning tradition was what grabbed me about Wildcat football. It was in junior high that I became aware of the winning tradition. I couldn't wait to get in those pants, blue front and white back. In junior high that's all we talked about." (Before his junior high days, he had followed Temple Dunbar High School where his older brother played. Integration came to Temple in 1963 and Dunbar closed in 1966.)

He continued about his playing time on the varsity, "It was all exciting. I just loved to play. In my junior year, we beat Abilene in non-district. My senior year we beat Bryan in Bryan. We were tied with Corsicana and I missed a chip shot field goal that cost us the district championship when we played them. But Coach McQueen called my number to kick a field goal against Bryan. I made it and it put the game out of reach for Bryan. It made me feel good that he had the confidence in me to kick again after I had missed an easy chip shot against Corsicana." I told him that his story sounded much like the one Doak Walker had written about his first three tries as a kicker for Highland Park when he missed his first two extra point attempts and just knew that that he had blown all his chances to ever kick again for the Scots. But just like McQueen had shown confidence in him, Walker's coach sent him back out there for a third chance which he made good on. Still, President and Walker remember those first missed kicks and feel bad that they initially didn't come through enough to where it was still a memory for them although they both got better and kicked well for their teams in later opportunities.

President continued, "Perhaps my best game came my junior year when we beat the Austin Maroons 17-10. I had a touchdown pass reception, a 37 yard field goal and two interceptions. The 37 yard field goal was the longest of my career." About McQueen, he commented, "I loved him for his honesty, his winning attitude and showing us how to win. His concern for us off the field was very important also. Finally, it was an honor when Coach McQueen asked me to wear #88 as my jersey number. That had been his old jersey number when he played for the Wildcats." President continues to live in Temple today where he works for CTWP.

Just like in so many other of the towns in Friday's Winners, there is one person who stands out as the voice of the local team either on the public address system or on the local radio show. In Temple, it is Gene Pemberton, a 1958 graduate of Temple High. He has been the color man since 1986 on KTEM-AM broadcasts of Temple football games. He and Mike McLain broadcasted together before McLain moved to bigger radio markets in east Texas. He is full of memories of past Wildcat players as well as learning who the new ones are as he prepares for his twenty-eighth year broadcasting the Wildcat games. They were recognized in 1993 by the Dallas Press Club as the winners of the Katie Award for the best small to medium market broadcasters in Texas. At the awards ceremony in Dallas, there was a playing of the memorable words he spoke very excitedly when the Wildcats recovered that fourth quarter fumble that ended Odessa Permian's last chance to win the 1992 non-district battle," MOJO JUST DIED!!!".

He played basketball in high school, but took up officiating football games for 23 years. He is an ordained minister, but mostly made his living for 32 years in sales for American Desk calling on schools for all kinds of athletic seating needs. He also spent 15 years as the chaplain of the Houston Astros, the only full time chaplain that any team had in MLB. I asked him about some of the most memorable Temple football players he had observed over the years. He mentioned Kenneth Davis, Brad Dusek and Lache Seastrunk. Always ready with a quip and a great story about Temple sports, he told about the incredible speed possessed by Seastrunk. I told him that I had been amazed at seeing the acceleration that Seastrunk could put on to run by defenders and then pull away from them. Pemberton responded, "I used to comment on the radio watching him turn the corner on a play and be three yards ahead at that point. Fifty yards later, the distance between him and the closest pursuer had grown to 10 yards. That's when I used the phrase, 'push the stopwatch' to describe what he was doing. When Temple played Belton in a game that was televised by ESPN, they had someone in the booth to pick up my saying that to go on the air. Unfortunately, Lache didn't have a run like that in that game, so it never got recorded."

Both McQueen and Pemberton mentioned Kenneth Davis as being among the best Wildcat ever; so I asked him for an interview and got a great response from him. He was on the Temple varsity from 1978 through 1980. McQueen saw the versatility of talent and skills he possessed and put him to work in a variety of positions to maximize his contributions to the team. Best known for his running back abilities, Davis also played left cornerback, punter, kick off and field goal kicker and kick returner. During his time there, Temple made it to the second round of the playoffs in his sophomore and senior years, but what was special was the State Championship they won in his junior year. The honors came to him accordingly. In his sophomore year he was Honorable Mention All-District as a cornerback. His junior year is when he pulled in a treasure trove of honors starting with first team All-District on both offense and defense. He was a Parade All-American as well as first team All-State. In his senior year when they only made it to the second round, Davis garnered first team All-District on offense and defense. He got a scholarship to play for TCU and was fifth in the Heisman Trophy voting in 1984. He had a ten-year professional career with the Green Bay Packers and the Buffalo Bills. He is one of only 19 players to be on four AFC championship teams with Buffalo.

Davis began by talking about the factor that made playing for Temple a special experience for him and all other Wildcats, "It was a small town with energy that fans brought to the stadium each week which was built up from the previous Friday night's game. The whole city embraced the game. It was part of the fabric of the town. People talked about it at coffee shops, etc. It was a community affair. You knew the players because they were your neighbors. There would be the 75 year old man who told you 'great game' in the grocery store, the 60 year old woman in church who would tell you what a great game we played. The small, young boy who would tell you he wanted to be just like you. We were a town with one heartbeat."

Then he talked about McQueen as his coach, "He believed in conditioning. He believed in you as a player. He surrounded himself with outstanding coaches. But most of all, he was a big man who carried a big stick. When he spoke, everyone went silent. He was a compassionate family man and brought the same qualities at home to the field. He was a man who believed in detail. He had confidence in the plays that the coaches were calling and the players would make the play. He was a coach about winning; winning was his stats. It wasn't about how many touchdowns were scored or yards were run; winning was his stats. He understood that every player was different and that's what made him such a great coach."

He remarked about playing in district games, "Every one of those games were significant. In my era, if you lost a district game, you didn't have a chance to make it to the playoffs because of the great rivalries. Bryan College Station—at the time both teams were undefeated and they came to Temple and we beat them. Another-in Waco playing University, kicked a 34 yard field goal in that game. It's so hard to single out significance of...because it was a team sport and every one of them counted. Bottom line was winning or losing. Didn't matter who had the best stats. You knew your number was going to be called and you wanted to rise to the occasion for whatever it might be."

Then Davis discussed the playoff games, " In 1978-playing Plano in Texas Stadium; lined up with clock running out. I lined up to kick a 56 yard field goal. Coach McQueen came up to me to say, 'Can you do it?' and I told him, 'I'll make it.' I walked out on the field and had no question in my mind that I could make it. When I kicked it, it came within two feet of the crossbar. One referee said it was good and the other said it was no good. Once we found out that it was no good, I cried and cried because my brother Earnest was a senior on that team and the seniors would not have any more opportunities to play high school football again. That's what hurt me the most."

His discussion moved to the playoffs in 1979, "Played Lewisville in Texas Stadium and we beat them 3-0. That was a huge win for us. It was something about that win that gave us momentum for the Plano game in Baylor Stadium. In the fourth quarter, we were down and Coach McQueen called 28 Sweet Victory Pass. What's ironic about the play; he had trusted me for the final play of the previous year and I didn't make it, but he trusted me again to catch this pass and I went up and caught the ball on the one yard line. We beat Plano and we then had all the confidence we needed to win the State Championship. We were hungry and it was something we carried every day with us in practice. When we finally met Spring Branch Memorial in Baylor Stadium, we were in a zone and felt we could win. When the game started it was like they were no match. We were hitting on all cylinders. I took a pitch on 28 Sweep and the line blocked so well that it ended up being a pile of players on the line. I jumped over the pile and ran it in for a touchdown. It was great to see all the Moms and Dads on the field after the game was over—how wonderful that was!" He mentioned that, "There were only two returning starters from the 1978 team that played on the 79 championship team, Vernon McVade and myself. In my high school career, the Temple record was 35-2."

Davis continues to promote the magic of playing on such a special team not only to players back in Temple, but also to players at Bishop Dunn Catholic School in Dallas where he is the athletic director. He concluded, "Yes, I let them know they are all together as one. Always remember one thing—it's 48 minutes to play and a lifetime to remember."

In the nine years after Bob McQueen retired, Temple football took a turn for the worse. There were three head coaches and only two winning seasons during that merry go round stretch. There was only one advancement to the second round of the playoffs. Temple gradually surrendered its position as the winningest high school football team in Texas back to the Amarillo Sandies. Records of 0-10 in 2005 and 1-9 in 2010 demonstrated just how much the Wildcats had derailed off the winning record track that was the hallmark of McQueen's reign. In all Temple had 32 wins and 62 losses during this period.

It was those losing numbers, the prior record of Temple and Mike Spradlin's tendency to gravitate to turnaround situations that caused him to apply for the job as head coach and athletic director when the Temple ISD board of trustees posted it for a fourth new coach before the 2011 season began. Spradlin had been a head coach at two UIL schools, Navasota and Round Rock Westwood between 1998 and 2002. During those years, his offenses had scoring averages per game in a season ranging from a low of 15.3 points to a high of 24.8 points per game. Then came the move where he remained a coach, but also became a student who apparently learned his lessons well. For he joined Art Briles' staff at the University of Houston for the 2003 through the 2005 seasons. That he took to the lessons of running a high scoring offense during that time with Briles became evident when he went back into coaching in the Texas public school spotlight again in 2006 at Abilene Cooper. Making the move to Cooper with him from Briles' UH staff was J.D. Berna.

His record at Cooper reflected that he had learned his lessons well and mimicked the improvement that Briles brought to Baylor University, including better season records spiced up by ever increasing offensive outputs. In his five years guiding the Cougars, Spradlin improved their record year by year from 4-6 in 2006 to 11-2 in 2010. The Cougar scoring per game leaped to 28.1 points in the first year, regressed back to 17.4 in the second year and then began soaring toward the stratosphere with leaps to 30.1 PPG in year three, 39.1 PPG in year four and a final season mark of 40.1 PPG for the Cooper Cougars.

Three years ago, he arrived at Temple to begin bringing back the legacy and tradition of winning Wildcat football. In 2011, they went 6-5 and averaged scoring 30.9 points a game. In 2012, they missed the playoffs as the third place team due to missing the tie breaker that determined who the third place representative from that district would be, but their scoring increased to an average of 36.8 points per game. In 2013, the Wildcats were back in the playoffs as district champions, showing that they had bought totally into Spradlin's scheme with a 44 point per game average, but lost a heartbreaking Bi-District clash 39-35 to the eventual Class 5A-DII state champion Cedar Hill. Temple led 28-7 at halftime in this season-ender that left the Wildcats with a 7-4 season record. To go along with the increased scoring output his team have had since he was associated with Briles, all seven of the years he has coached since then, his teams have averaged over 500 yards total offense a game.

When I went to his office at Wildcat Stadium for an interview, I got a quick look at the varsity dressing area and assistant coaches' office space before he ended a staff meeting to come take me to his office. Wildcat colors are royal blue and white with the royal blue dominating the color scheme of the area for the players. In the locker room is a big mural covering one wall floor to ceiling and end to end that has pictures of groups of Wildcat players from different teams. In the middle of the picture mural is the phrase, "48 minutes to play, a lifetime to remember."

Off to the side is a board that gives information on each district game coming up in 2014. The opponents are named, mascots, players by position, their all-district players, location and date of the game. On another wall above some of the player lockers are boards reminding the Wildcats of their goals on offense, defense and special teams. For each game, a player can be named the top player in categories such as MVP, Big Nasty, Big Stick and Hard Hat. Pictures of the Wildcat players chosen by the coaches for each honor go up on the board on a week by week basis as the season progresses. Each of the lockers has a big block T sign in it. The players who are returning from last year's squad already have their names up on the locker they are assigned. The fact that there were so many lockers unnamed yet was a reminder that two-a-days that would help the coaches determine whose names were going up were still 10 days away from beginning. Finally, as you pass into the assistant coaches desk area, there was a sign reminding the players there were "only two rules to Wildcat defense; one: get your butt to the football; two: be PISSED Off when you get there!"

I finally got the chance to meet Mike Spradlin for the first time and he began to talk about the Wildcats, his coaching strategy and what makes it tick for him. Spradlin commented on his progress to date at Temple, "Getting past the first round is definitely our goal. The group of players that we have now is our first group made up entirely of Wildcat players that have only been coached by our staff." That he is happy to be there along with Brena who came from Cooper with him to be the assistant Temple head coach and strength coach is voiced in his statement, "Temple is an amazing community, full of great people and great tradition."

Already there are several games from his first three years at the Wildcat helm, a stretch that he would like to see end when it is finally time for him to retire, that are special memories to him. The most exciting game was, Spradlin exclaimed, "The 51-35 win over Copperas Cove in 2013. It was the first Temple win in 10 years!" He continued on about the 2013 season, "We beat Killeen High School in the last game of the regular season 63-42 for the district championship. The biggest game overall has been the 39-35 loss to Cedar Hill in Bi-District in 2013."

There is one player on the Wildcats who stand out as the top offensive player on the team. He says, "Chad President, our current quarterback, has tremendous passion, leadership and work ethic." President is returning to the quarterback position after a season ending ACL injury on the first play of the third game of 2013. In the first two games, President had accounted for nearly 900 yards of total offense. He has committed to play for Briles at quarterback at Baylor after his senior year at Temple.

As for the 2014 Temple season, Spradlin says, "We should have a good year. We are returning an 1800 yard runner (Jeff Carr) and a 900 yard rusher (Marques Hatcher)." The Wildcats are picked to be the district champions again, this time in the newly realigned District 17-5A. I definitely got a feeling as I left Wildcat Stadium that this team could very well be playing in the Class 5A, DI state championship game in December.

THE TYLER JOHN TYLER LIONS

FIRST YEAR THEY PLAYED: 1908
ALL-TIME RECORD THROUGH 2013: 671-361-41
PERCENTAGE: 63.96%
PLAYOFF APPEARANCES: 33
STATE CHAMPIONSHIP GAMES WON: 1930, 1973, 1994
STATE CHAMPIONSHIP GAMES LOST: 1955, 2000

CUJO. It's a word that has been used with pride around Tyler High School for 33 years. But why? What does it mean? Probably the best-known version of CUJO is as the name of a horror tale written by Stephen King, which later became a movie. It was 1983 when CUJO got introduced to the world as the family pet St. Bernard that became a man-killer after he was bitten by a rabid bat. That hardly seems to be a basis for making this word as an inspiration and source of pride for the 5A Tyler Lions. Further searches for its definition finally led to one that says it is an Indian word meaning an indomitable spirit. In other words, the Lions never quit, never die when they're on the athletic fields. I visited with the former offensive coordinator of the Lions, Antoine Bush, to get that meaning given to me. Bush is a young coach having just graduated from Tyler High in 2005. If there is anyone who should know what Cujo means, it is Bush. Or it is the Lions' head coach, Ricklen Holmes. He is a 1998 graduate of Tyler John Tyler High School. Both those coaches have been steeped in the tradition of CUJO and embrace its role in the success on the football field of the Lions.

To heighten the impact of CUJO on the Lions varsity team, the word only comes out for regular usage by the team once they have made the playoffs. What happens then is the total immersion of the team in CUJO. The varsity players get new blue and white jerseys with two big changes on them from the jerseys they had been wearing during the regular season. On the front of the jersey in big menacing letters across the chest is CUJO. On the back of the jersey is the player's surname just above the number. That's normally only seen on college jerseys. So how well does CUJO work for the Lions? Since it came into being 30 years ago, Tyler has advanced to the playoffs 18 times. So while it does provide inspiration and build their spirits, CUJO is helped along by the immense talent and work ethic of the Lions. And they have been doing that long before CUJO appeared on the scene. In the 106 years Tyler has fielded a team, it has been in the playoffs 33 times. State championship trophies for 1930, 1973 and 1994 grace the trophy cases.

But 50 years before CUJO became a part of the Tyler tradition, the Lions became the first team in East Texas to win a state title. It was 1930 and the Lions overcame the Amarillo Sandies, who were in their first year of being coached by Blair Cherry. The teams played for the State Championship and Tyler won 25-13. They were coached by George Foltz to a 13-0-1 record that year. The Lions beat Greenville 26-6 in Bi-District and Austin 44-0 in the Semi-Finals. For the year, they scored 345 points and gave up only 64 points. Foltz coached at Tyler for eight years and compiled a 56-21-4 record.

The next time that Tyler appeared in a State Championship game was in 1955. Leading the Lions on the field then was Charles F. Milstead. He was the quarterback and a safety. Red Stidger commented, "it was like having an offensive coordinator and defensive coordinator on the field when he was out there." He played on the Tyler varsity in 1954, 1955 and 1956. In the playoffs in 1955, Tyler beat Corpus Christi Miller 28-0 in Bi-District and Baytown Lee 22-7 in the Semi-Finals. Then they met the defending state champion Abilene Eagles in the 4A State Champion game. Tyler was favored to upend the Eagles, but lost 33-13. Milstead was All-District his sophomore and junior years. In his senior year, he added to those honors All-State, All-Texas, All-Southern, All-American and was voted captain of the Lions and MVP of the team. He got a scholarship to play at Texas A & M, then played professionally. He says of his time playing for Tyler, "Playing at Tyler opened the door for a college education for me."

Johnny "Red" Stidger is considered one of the most beloved coaches the Lions have ever had. In the chapter on Amarillo High, he was one of the first people profiled for being the quarterback of the Sandies in 1934 when they won their first State Championship. He played at SMU and went into the oil business after college. Stidger worked for American Liberty Pipeline Company for 11 years. But when it came time for him to transfer to its South Texas location, he didn't want to leave East Texas, so he went into coaching starting at Spring Hill in 1949. He finished his education at Stephen F. Austin in Nacogdoches. In 1958 he took over as Tyler's head coach. He coached there for the next 11 years retiring after the 1968 season. His only team that made the playoffs was his 1959 edition of the Lions. The Lions were 7-2-2 that year losing to Highland Park 41-6 in the Bi-District match.

Three times in this stretch, the Lions tied for district, only to lose the coin flip to determine which team would advance to the playoffs each time. Stidger said that Texarkana was the toughest team in his district to beat. A key player for the Lions when they were to meet Texarkana in the 1964 game was quarterback Alan Flynn. Flynn broke his collar bone during Open Week practice and had to miss the game.

That 1964 season produced his best single season record as the Lions went 9-1. His 11 year total as Tyler's head coach was 68-36-7. Asked which players that he had coached 45 to 55 years ago still stand out to him as the most outstanding, Stidger quickly replied, "On offense, it was Billy Hayes. He was the quarterback on the 1962 and 1963 teams. He could have played anywhere. He would have helped if he had played on defense." As for a defensive standout, Stidger said, "That was Earl Maxfield. He was a big guy, weighted about 245 pounds. He could move and loved contact. He actually played both ways as a linebacker and as an offensive tackle."

He continued about all the players that played for the Lions while he coached, "I had a good string of football players then. They were all good kids. I was glad to have had a chance to coach them." His 'kids' as he calls them are now in their late 60s, early 70s. Yet their affection for the man who coached them and taught them life lessons still prevails today. Those who still live in the Tyler area have been regular visitors to see him several times a month to this day. He retired from coaching about two years too early to have the privilege of coaching the greatest player the Lions ever had, the Tyler Rose. Earl Campbell began playing at Tyler High about 1970. Stidger says of Campbell, "He was the toughest player I have ever seen. It would have been fun to have coached him."

Stidger was asked about the games he coached that were the most meaningful to him. Candidly he replied, "The ones with Tyler Robert E. Lee. Initially it was ugly as it could get. The Tyler High kids were the underprivileged kids, but we had the football players. The Tyler Lee kids had the money. "The student body of Tyler High was split to create the enrollment at Tyler Lee. That happened the same year of 1958 when Stidger began to coach there. He continued, "They didn't have as many students, so Lee became a 3A school while we were still a 4A school. But we opened our season each year playing the Rebels. For the first five years, it was a non-district game. Then they grew to be a 4A school and we were in the same district. It was a good series when I coached. The best game might have been one where the Lions lost to the Rebels 14-13 in 1965."

Integration came to Tyler in the late 1960s and the Lions began to get the great athletes who had previously played for Emmet Scott High School. The school closed in 1970 under court order for the Tyler schools to be integrated. Corky Nelson arrived to coach the Lions about the same time that Earl Campbell joined the Lion varsity. Campbell played defense as a sophomore and junior. Nelson put him at running back for his senior year and the rest is history. The Lions went 15-0-0 and won the Class 4A State Championship. They scored 399 points and ceded 99 to the opposition. In the playoffs, Tyler rolled past Plano 34-0 in Bi-District, Conroe 10-7 in Regional, Fort Worth Arlington Heights 34-17 in the Quarter-Finals, Arlington Houston 22-7 in the Semi-Finals and Austin Reagan 21-14 for the State Championship. It was said by those who watched Campbell playing for the Lions that he could have gone directly into the NFL from high school, the only person given that tribute. However he played for Texas University and won the Heisman Trophy in 1977, one of the two players from schools in this book to get that honor along with Doak Walker of Highland Park who won it at SMU in 1948.

About Earl, the playoff game in which he prevailed was the Regional game against Conroe. For one thing, he threw a pass in the game on the winning drive. It was for 18 yards to quarterback Larry Hartsfield. More importantly, he carried the ball nine times in the 13-play drive. I have read a number of people's accounts who were there to see the game in person who said that there were as many as five Conroe Tigers hanging on to Earl on each carry as he kept lifting his powerful legs to forge ahead. Finally he went the final five yards for the go-ahead score with 2:04 left in the game. Of course, it has become legend how he played only as a linebacker for the Lions during his first two years on the varsity, then finally asked his coach if he could try carrying the ball. As Red Stidger said, "After that tryout, he was the ball carrier from then on." In his senior year, he averaged 225 yards per game rushing on the way to a 15-0 record and the 4A state championship. In the chapter titled Recognition, Earl is listed as a Parade Magazine All-American for the 1973 team.

Coach Allen Wilson who directed successful football programs at three different high schools had his best success at the second of the three schools he led, the Tyler Lions. He came to Tyler in 1991 from Paris where he coached the school to the 4A 1988 state championship. In Tyler, he never had a losing season in 11 years between 1991 and 2001. There were only three of those 11 seasons when the Lions didn't advance into the playoffs. In all at Tyler, his record was 102-34-2, right at a 75% success rate. Coach Wilson's most successful period at Tyler were the four years from 1994 through 1997 when he went 51-6 and the Lions captured the 1994 5A, Division I State Championship with a 16-0 record. In 1995, the Lions reached the Area round. The next year, they reached the Quarter-Finals knocking out the Temple Wildcats 54-24 in the Regional round. In 1997, they advanced to the Semi-Finals.

Wilson in 28 years compiled a 246-90-4 coaching record at Paris, Tyler and Dallas Carter. He had only one losing season at Paris in his 28 years. He retired after 10 seasons at Carter. But a recent statement he made about his profession sounds as if he still considers himself on the field, and in the locker room making a difference in the lives of the young men he coaches. He said, "There are very few professions in our society that afford a person an opportunity to make a difference in the lives of young people. Coaching provides multiple opportunities to do just that. Through coaching, attitudes are changed, discipline is instilled, good habits are established and life chances are enhanced. Coaches have the opportunity and the platform to deal hope."

He continued, "Good coaches not only focus on teaching essential knowledge and skills of their individual sport, they also spend a great deal of time instilling intangible qualities within the life of athletes. I am proud to be a coach and honored to be remembered by a former player. I coach because I love the game, and I see it as an opportunity to use my God-given talents and abilities to minister to young men, change lives and provide a positive contribution to society."

Asked about the games that were outstanding to him at Tyler, he first mentioned the playoff game with Plano East in 1994. It was the Regional Semi-Final 5A-DII game in Texas Stadium. Both schools came into the game with 12-0 records and top five in the state polls ratings. Plano East was #2 and Tyler #3. There were 20,000 fans there to cheer for the teams. The game started out tamely enough with the Panthers and Lions tied 7-7 after one quarter. At the half, Tyler John Tyler had a 21-14 lead. The two schools each added a field goal to their totals in the third quarter. Then came the fourth quarter, the last half of which would go into the record books and into football lore for the fireworks the two teams would produce in that short time span.

The Lions added a field goal early in the fourth quarter for a 27-17 lead. As the Panthers were driving for a score with less than five minutes left to play, a Lions player stripped the ball from the Panther quarterback at the Tyler 10 yard line. The fumble recovery was run back 90 yards for the score with 4:24 on the clock. A little over a minute later, the Lions took still another recovered Panther fumble to the house for a 41-17 lead with 3:03 left in the game.

While many fans left the stadium to get to their cars early certain that the game was settled, down on the field, the Panthers were just getting started on making a comeback for the ages. They drove 70 yards in two plays to score with 2:36 to go in the game. The missed two point conversion left the score 41-23, Tyler. The Panthers executed successfully three onside kick recoveries in a row in the time remaining and scored a touchdown each time within six plays of the recoveries. They were good on the first two point conversion to pull within 10 points of the Lions at 41-31 with 1:29 left to play. The Panthers were back in the end zone within 33 seconds after their second onside kick, but missed the two point conversion. The score was 41-37 with 56 seconds left in the game. It took the Panthers three plays after the third successful onside kick to score and take the lead 44-41 with 24 seconds left in the game.

The radio announcers for the game, Eddie Clinton and Denny Garver along with special guest to the radio booth, Lake Highlands head coach Mike Zoffuto, were going crazy calling the game as it evolved. Zoffuto was there to scout the two teams as his Highlands team would play the winner the following week in the Regional final. It seemed that luck and redemption played a hand in what happened in the next 13 seconds of the game. Plano East kicked off to the Lion three yard line. Roderick Dunn fielded the kick. He had missed grabbing the ball on the last two onside kicks, setting the Panthers up for their comeback. This time, there was no stopping Dunn as he blasted for 97 yards and the winning touchdown with 11 seconds left in the game.

The broadcast of that game as well as the video showing the game have become classics that can be aired or shown these days to anyone with a computer. Clinton and Garver got their 15 minutes of fame as they made appearances on the Tonight Show with Jay Leno. The broadcast won the 1995 ESPY for the Showstopper of the Year. Recently former Lion assistant coach David Clapp told me there is a chance that the story of the game will be made into a movie. Keep this story in mind when you read about current coach Ricklan Holmes and what happened in the 2012 Class 4A, DI Semi-Final game further on in this chapter.

I asked Coach Wilson to name a key district game he coached at Tyler and he replied the 1995 matchup with Longview won by the Lions 28-7. He had three players he singled out for their play with the Lions while he coached there. He began, " Morris Anderson and Mickey Jones, both of these young men played QB. They were outstanding leaders, tough-minded, play-makers. They had poise under pressure."

Anderson was a quarterback from 1991, Wilson's first season there, through 1994. Jones played from 1993 through 1996. On defense, Wilson cited David Warren stating, "He was a mentally tough athlete with speed and size to run to the football. He had great quickness for a defensive end." I listed Warren in the Recognition chapter for being named an All-American player by USA Today magazine. There is more to his credentials than just my notation of him making the list. According to USA Today, which chose him for the 1996 team, he was the National High School

Defensive Player of the Year. Among his stats listed in a Wikipedia write up about him, Warren caught a touchdown pass and returned one of the two recovered fumbles for a score in the Plano East game. As a sophomore that year, he had 106 tackles and six sacks. His junior year in 1995, he made 126 tackles, 18 sacks and four blocked punts. In his senior year, he was double-teamed and triple-teamed quite a bit by blockers for the other teams, but still managed 106 tackles and eight and a half sacks. He played at Florida State after he graduated.

Coach David K. Clapp was a member of Wilson's staff at Tyler from 1994 to 2002. In speaking to him for the first time, he told me how he and two other coaches were always on Wilson's staff at Paris, Tyler and Dallas Carter. The chemistry that the four of them had together as a coaching staff was readily picked up by the players on their teams. His remarks reminded me that two players in *Friday's Winners* had said much the same thing about the men who coached them and were part of a staff that stayed together for more than 25 years. They both attributed at least a part of their team's successes to the fact that a coaching staff that stays together for decades were leading their teams. Jimmy Carmichael of Brownwood spoke highly of the trio headed by Gordon Wood, who coached the Lions for 28 years. Likewise, Sterling Elza was just as high on the six men who remained on Larry Dippel's staff at Amarillo High for more than 30 years.

Clapp said that he was drawn to Tyler by its tradition and expectation of winning state championships. The two games that provided the most exciting wins for him were the 1994 Plano East game and beating Austin Westlake 35-24 in the Dome for the State Championship that year. As far as district games go, Clapp said, "The biggest games were every Longview game we played." As for the top players he coached, he mentioned Marc Broyles, Michael Price and Mickey Jones as offensive stars. He said, "They were always clutch players when the game was in doubt." He cited the same three players plus Warren as being the defensive standouts. By the way, Clapp is not related to Kenneth Clapp who coached at Amarillo High.

If you have ever met Tyler head coach Ricklan Holmes, then you probably know about his passion for the Lions and what he expects them to accomplish each season, no less than a state championship. It was that way the first day I met him on July 12, 2012. It was to be his first season as the head coach at his alma mater from which he graduated in 1998. He had been on the varsity teams coached by Allen Wilson for the four seasons that began with the Lions winning their most recent championship in 1994. In my recent interview of him, Holmes stated, "I was raised in Tyler, Texas and competed at Tyler John Tyler High School in both football and track." He wanted to coach where he attended school. When I met him, he told me then that he expected Tyler to win the Class 4A, DI State Championship for 2012. I was taken by his very positive attitude, but somewhat uncertain if it would turn out that way.

The Lions nearly played for the State Championship, but lost the shootout that was the State Semi-Final game to eventual State Champion Denton Guyer 57-53. The game was played at Midlothian Stadium on December 14, 2012. In the portion of this chapter that I wrote about Coach Allen White, I covered the 1994 game between Tyler and Plano East which was a classic shootout ending in the 48-44 Tyler victory.

In that game, Plano East rallied in the final three minutes to score four touchdowns and recovered three onside kicks in a row to wipe out a 41-17 Tyler lead and go up 44-41 with 24 seconds left in the game. At Midlothian Stadium, the Lions were in much the same shape as Plano East trailing Guyer 50-31 with six minutes left in the game. It seemed to be déjà vu all over again with the Lions having learned from Plano East how to affect a comeback in this manner. In 74 seconds, Tyler came up with 22 points as the Lions successfully executed two onside kick recoveries. Quarterback Greg Ward completed a 65 yard touchdown pass as Tyler moved in front of Guyer 53-50 with 3:44 left in the game.

Tyler succeeded in its offense on the arm of Ward who completed 46 of 64 passes for 544 yards and five touchdowns. Guyer intercepted three of his passes, one more than he had been picked the entire season in all the previous games. He also ran for 108 yards and one touchdown. While Tyler succeeded through the air, Guyer prospered on the ground. The Wildcats rushed for 612 yards on 61 carries. They got the go-ahead touchdown to barely pull out a 57-53 win and go on to win state, the first of two years in a row to get the title.

So as I interviewed Coach Holmes for the 2014 season, I was not surprised this time to have him say that he expected the Lions to first win their new district 16-5A despite the pigskin prognosticators choosing them to finish second behind Ennis, and then that they would again play for and win the State Championship. He stated, "We have depth, great football players and experience."

Asked about his coaching record at Tyler after two years, he responded, "I am very pleased with all 20 wins we have so far" He also said that all four of the wins the Lions got in 2012 in the playoffs before meeting Guyer were very special to him. His record is 20-6 after the two seasons. He closed mentioning the players he has coached that he considers the best to date. His offensive choice is Ward, now a quarterback for the University of Houston, "He is a great athlete and an outstanding player." On the defensive side of the ball, Holmes picked out two former players as being the best, "Chris Hackett, a strong safety at TCU and Triston Wade, a free safety at UTSA. These are equally great athletes and outstanding leaders." With that enthusiasm for the Lions, Coach Holmes could very well motivate his talented squad to go all the way.

WHEN PATHS CROSSED

With so many of the top winning teams located in the same vicinity, there have been many games played between most of the dozen schools. Particularly those schools in fairly close geographic location to one another. When it came playoff time, even the teams not very close to the center of the state came together in epic clashes, often with the state title on the line. Some of these games have gone down in the record books as classic gridiron battles.

Listing only the games that determined a state championship that involved two of the top twelve winning teams is a short list. Some of the playoff games over the years that determined what team was going to state were very special. There are a number of those to recall. There are others that are just regular season rivalry clashes that should be noted also. To begin, here are the games that decided a state championship. In 1930, Tyler beat Amarillo 25-13. In 1940, Amarillo defeated Temple 20-7 in the Cotton Bowl before 18,000 spectators. In 1948, the UIL began classifying teams into three classes-City, 2A, 1A. Some 22 years later, the UIL had expanded to four classes-4A, 3A, 2A, 1A. In 1970, Brownwood blanked Cuero 14-0 for the title in 3A.

There have been seventy-two other games in the playoffs between members of the distinguished dozen. Plano has been in the most games-seventeen to date. The Wildcats are 10-7 in a thirty-one year period between 1970 and 2000. Temple has an 8-5 mark in thirteen games played between 1938 and 2011. Tyler began an eleven game series of playoff games between the others in the book in 1930 and has a 6-5 mark going through 2011. Splitting eight games to create a 4-4 record is Highland Park. In their first year of competition in 1923, the Scots defeated Longview 20-0. In a 2011 game, they were edged out by the Tyler John Tyler Lions 42-39 to drop to the 4-4 record. The Longview Lobos have four wins in eleven games going back to that 1923 loss to the Scots 20-0 and ending with a 24-3 Bi-District win over Temple in 2011.

The rest of the teams have been in five or less games involving the schools making their way into Friday's Winners. Cuero has a 3-2 mark that began in 1942 with a Bi-District loss to Hondo 27-12 and ended with a 1994 win over Hondo in Bi-District 49-6. Brownwood has a 2-2 mark. The Lions beat Plano 35-21 in the 1970 Semi-Finals. Then they knocked off Cuero for the State Championship 14-0 the next week. A year later, they met Plano again in the State Semi-Finals, but lost 10-8 this time. Thirty-three years later, they lost to Corsicana 38-21 in the Area round in 2004. Hondo has played against Cuero three times in the playoffs between 1942 and 1994. In a close Area game in 1986, the Owls lost to the Gobblers 18-15 to compile a 1-2 record to date.

That's the same record compiled by Cameron Yoe so far. The Yoemen beat Mart 15-13 in Bi-District in 1936. In 1946, the Panthers got them back 46-0 in a Regional contest which was as far as the smaller teams could play then. In 1987, Cuero edged them in the state Semi-Finals 34-27. Amarillo has gone 2-2 beginning with a 33-25 win over the Corsicana Lions in the 1930 Semi-Finals, but lost to Tyler 25-13 in the State Championship game the next week. In 1940 came the 20-7 win over Temple for the state title. Fifty–two years later in 1992, the Sandies lost to Temple 38-7 in the State Semi-Finals. Mart is 1-1 losing to Cameron 15-13 in Bi-District in 1936. Then came the 46-0 win over Cameron in Regional in 1946. Corsicana has two wins in two games. The first came in 1931 with a 33-25 Semi-Final win over Tyler. It would be seventy-four years later before the Tigers faced another top dozen foe, beating Brownwood 38-21 in the 2004 Area game.

Three of these games stand out as shootouts with the last team having the ball being the winner. Highland Park played in two of them losing both times. In 1977, the Scots lost to Plano 29-28 in the state 4A Quarter-Finals. In 2011, the Scots lost to Tyler 42-39 in the 4A Regional playoff game. The third game was the 1987 3A Semi-Final match in which Cuero came out on top 34-27 over Cameron Yoe.

In 1977, the Scots seemed to have the Quarter-Final game played at Texas Stadium under control as they led Plano 28-0 in the third quarter. Lance McIlhenny, the Highland Park quarterback, had figured in all the scoring plays as he passed for two scores and ran for two more, the last run for two yards building the four touchdown lead. The Wildcats were led by their quarterback, Steve Ulmer in the thrilling rally as he scored on a run and then passed for another touchdown to cut the Scot lead to 28-14. The Plano defense accounted for the next score in the game as Carl Smith intercepted McIlhenny's pitchout and went all the way for the score. The final score came when Ulmer passed for a sixty-one yard touchdown with only thirty three seconds left in the game. He kept the ball for a two point conversion and Plano's first lead in the game. The

Wildcats kept the Scots from doing any more to rally back and advanced to the state Semi-Final game the following week with an amazing 29-28 win.

Cuero was on a roll in 1987 having played for the State Championship the previous two years. Over that three year stretch, the Gobblers had won 43 of 46 games coming into the Semi-Final game against the Cameron Yoe Yoemen. Cuero was 14-0 for the season and the Yoe had a 13-0 record. Under coach Toby York, Cameron had seventy-seven wins in seven years, including the 1981 State Championship in his first year at the helm. Leading the offense of Gobbler head coach Pat Blessing was the great running back Robert Strait. He had rumbled for 3,071 yards on 310 carries and 51 rushing touchdowns in the first fourteen games. He had scored 350 points total. Now he was 89 yards shy of being third on the all time single season rushing totals among all Texas high school running backs. But the Gobblers also had Wayne Mathis at quarterback and he was very proficient leading the offense. He had rushed for nine touchdowns and passed for 16 touchdowns when he wasn't handing the ball to Strait to work his magic.

For Cameron, quarterback Paul Johnson led the way for the first thirteen games, but it was doubtful that he would play in this game due to an ankle injury he had suffered in the 13-0 Quarter-Final win over Corrigan-Camden the week before. It was thought that the trio of running backs who each had decent rushing stats might be the game plan for Cameron. That trio consisted of Freddie Townsend, James Whitehead and Mike Bradley.

The stage was set for the December 12 meeting at Memorial Stadium in Austin. For the winner, there would be a berth to meet the McGregor Bulldogs the next week at Memorial Stadium for the Class 3A State Championship. As might be expected, there was no way that Johnson would miss this game. And sure enough, he played and played well enough to keep the Yoemen in the game. Cuero scored first on a one yard plunge by Strait and an extra point conversion by Johnny Blackwell with 7:52 left in the first quarter. Johnson made a 56 yard pass to Townsend a minute later for the Yoemen. Then Townsend scored on a one yard run. Craig Bethell tied the game at the 6:20 mark with his extra point. After Cameron recovered the onside kick, the Yoemen took the lead 10-7 on a 32 yard field goal by Bethell at the 2:50 mark of the opening period. Not to be outdone, Cuero scored on a 25 yard pass from Mathis to Jason Gonzales with 1:29 on the clock, still in the first period.

Cameron dominated the second quarter. Johnson hit Aaron Barrett with a five yard touchdown pass. Bethell made his second 32 yard field goal of the game on the final play of the first half. The Yoemen defense had helped by holding Strait to 34 yards on eight totes in the first half. The Gobblers made the adjustments and took over the game in the third quarter. They were down

20-14 when Strait became the go to player. He carried the ball 27 times in the second half good for 197 yards and touchdown runs of two and 81 yards. He carried in a two point conversion. He finished the game with 231 yards on 35 carries and three touchdowns plus the two point conversion.

Cuero tied the game at 20-20 as Mathis threw a five yard scoring strike to Carlos Taylor. A short 17 yard punt by Bethell set up the Gobblers for a 35 yard drive to take the lead for good early in the fourth quarter. Strait scored on the two yard run and added the two point conversion for a 28-20 lead with 7:51 left in the game. Trooper Taylor picked off a Johnson pass, his only interception in a 15 for 29 performance for 297 yards on his bad ankle. Strait took a pitch and raced around left end for an 81 yard run with 3:56 left in the game. The extra point kick was missed. Bradley scored on a one yard run to get Cameron closer. Bethell added the extra point, but the Gobblers had the 34-27 win in hand. The next week, back at Memorial Stadium, they beat the McGregor Bulldogs 14-6 for the State crown. Strait carried 39 more times for 213 yards and a season total of 3515 yards, second on the all time list for a single season.

The Tyler-Highland Park game took place in Waco on November 26, 2011, in the third round of the playoffs. Scott Ellerman replaced the injured Brad Burgin at quarterback for the Scots. At the half, the Scots led 24-21. Preston Miller of Highland Park had gained 77 of the yards on an 80 yard drive for the Scots. Jackson Hansen scored on a three yard dive to complete the drive. Tyler came back as Fred Ross rumbled 47 yards for a touchdown. Then Tyler Lion quarterback Greg Ward blasted 66 yards for another Tyler score. Justin Liggins went 39 yards for another score. Tyler pulled out the 42-39 win. Coincidentally on that same date, Corsicana beat Frisco Centennial 52-31 in the 4A, DII Regional Semi-Final as Cameron Washington ran for 214 yards and four touchdowns. That set a new season rushing record for Corsicana beating Ketric's old record of 2761 yards set in 1994. Washington ended the season with 3210 yards rushing.

That 29-28 comeback win by Plano in 1977 over Highland Park was just one of ten playoff games played between five of the teams in *Friday's Winners* in the period of 1976 through 1986. It was a period that built rivalries and displayed why these teams belong in *Friday's Winners*. That's because most of the games were played in the second round and beyond of the playoffs, demonstrating the staying power that allowed them to be in the dozen teams that have the most wins in Texas high school football history. Only two of the 10 games were played in the Bi-District round.

The other teams in the quintet are Temple, Longview and Tyler. In 1976, the Scots lost to the Temple Wildcats in the Quarter-Finals 28-14. In 1978.

Tyler and Plano tied 13-13 in Bi-District. Plano advanced because the Wildcats had the most first downs. Plano played Temple the next week in the Regional game and won it 15-14. In 1979, Temple got payback, beating Plano 19-16 in the Regional game.

In the 1980 playoffs, Plano met three of the teams in three consecutive weeks. The Wildcats beat Longview 23-7 in Bi-District, beat Temple 16-0 in Regional and lost to Highland Park 23-21 in the Quarter-Finals. It would be three years before there would be another matchup. Plano beat Temple 20-14 in the Regional game in 1983. The Scots got their second playoff win in a row over the Wildcats with a 17-7 win in the 1984 Area game. Finally, Plano beat the Longview Lobos 17-12 in the 1986 Quarter-Finals.

So in 2014 with the realignment by the UIL creating the new 6A class, which of these teams might cross paths in the playoffs? The first game of the season saw Plano losing to Tyler John Tyler 30-12. In the second game, Tyler beat Longview 41-25. In 16-5A district play, Corsicana played Tyler on October 24.

Amarillo in 2-6A, Plano in 6-6A and Highland Park in 10-6A moved to the new highest classification. In addition to Corsicana and Tyler, Longview and Temple are in Class 5A, playing in 15-5A and 17-5A respectively. Brownwood is in 3-4A-Div I. In 4A-Div II is Hondo in District 13 and Cuero in District 15. Cameron Yoe will be playing in 10-3A-Div I. Mart from 8-2A, Div I is expected to play for the State Championship, probably against Refugio, a team that is getting close to the bottom levels of wins by the top dozen teams profiled here.

SCORING BIG, DOMINATING ON DEFENSE

This chapter came about because Bryan Moore, the associate superintendent of the Groesbeck Independent School District in charge of the financial side of the operations, told me that there was only one school for me to write about based on their scoring numbers on offense and defense. The 1983 Daingerfield Tigers won the Class 3A State Championship with a 16-0 record. What's more, they scored 631 points and held their opponents to only eight points for the season. Pretty impressive until I began researching among my 12 schools to see who might have been close to numbers like that on both sides of the ball. Right off the bat, I found the 1927 Longview Lobos finished the year 10-0-1. In doing so, the Lobos put up 479 points and gave up only two points for the year, a safety to Mineola in a 78-2 win. So doing the math to see which school had the best stats, I came up with Longview averaging 43.54 points per game while giving up only .181 points per game. Daingerfield averaged ONLY 39.43 points per game while allowing exactly a half point per game, nearly three times as much as Longview. Sorry about that Bryan.

Of course, he will point out that Longview only played 11 games and didn't get a State Championship. Perhaps he might have had a point there. I looked to see that Waco High was the '27 State Champion defeating Abilene according to Texas Football magazine. It made me wonder why Longview didn't get to play Waco for the State Championship if there was only one class for all Texas high school football teams that year. So I asked Joe Lee Smith if he had an explanation for how that came about. What he explained to me is a good primer on the development of the playoff system by the UIL over the years.

The UIL came into being for football competition in 1920. Through 1926, all schools were in one division playing for the State Championship. There were no districts. But there were about 300 high schools assigned to sections depending on their location, about 20 schools per section. The teams had to play at least five schools in their section by early November. The UIL matched the remaining undefeated section schools against each other in games until there was only one left to represent the section in a state tournament. There were about 16 teams left to play in the state tournament.

Around 1922, the UIL separated the small and large schools in a section into A and B teams. Then in 1926-1927, the schools were divided into A and B classes by enrollment. The cutoff number might have been 300 students. The A teams played for a State Championship. The B teams played for a Bi-District championship. That enrollment number for Longview being under 300 in 1927 was the reason the Lobos didn't play the 300+ student enrollment Waco Lions for the state championship.

In 1928 through 1938, the UIL continued the Class A schools in the same format, but moved the B schools into competition for a Regional championship. Class C was formed for the smallest schools, but without a playoff system, just district competition only. In 1938, the UIL began six man football with playoff competition. In 1939, Class A became Class AA and class B became Class A. Class C became Class B with a Bi-District championship being the furthest a school could go in competition. This status prevailed until 1947 when Class A began playing for a State Championship and Class B for a Regional championship.

In 1948 to 1950, the UIL added the Big City conference consisting of schools from Dallas, Fort Worth, Houston and San Antonio. There were only four districts in the Big City Conference. So they played a Bi-District game and then the State Championship game. In 1951, 4A and 3A came into existence. In 1980, 5A was added. In 2014, there will be a 6A class for the first time. Of course, Division I and Division II came in beginning at the 5A level in 1990.

With that explanation of how the UIL gradually created the classes of competition, let me get back to naming those schools that scored a bunch while minimizing points by their opponents. I decided that one school outscoring its opponents in a season by a total score of 400+ points to 100 or less points fit the bill of one dominating. You will see as you read through the lists that there are fewer and fewer teams that have been able to hold their opponents to 100 or fewer points in recent seasons. You can blame that on the evolution of the spread offense which definitely has leveled the playing field in that respect. On the other hand, there are several teams that have put up even more staggering scores that their opponents have been unable to stop, given the effectiveness of the spread.

Here are the teams that have achieved that 400-100 point difference in a season. Amarillo in 1928 went 9-2 and had a scoring margin of 509-57. The

Scoring Big, Dominating on Defense

1930 Sandies were 12-1 with a 419-95 margin. The 1931 Sandies were 10-2-0 scoring 424 points to 62 points. The 1936 Sandies were 14-0-0 with a margin of 455 to 66 points. The 1957 Amarillo team were 11-1-0 with 470 points to 69 points.

Brownwood in 1962 went 11-1-0 scoring 414 points and allowing 82 points. Then in 2010, the Lions scored 801 points while compiling a 14-1-0 record. The Cameron Yoe Yoemen didn't have any games like that on defense, but scored 645 points in 2010 and 699 points in 2013, both state championship teams. Corsicana had four seasons putting up 400-100 numbers: 1930, 11-1-0 with 447-72, 1931, 12-1-0 with 451 to 64, 1949, 10-1-0 with 402 points to 98 points and 1950-9-1-0 with 409-16.

Cuero has stood out with two seasons of scoring above 600 points-695 in the 16-0-0 1987 state championship year and 660 in the 12-3-0 2007 season. During the magic 44 game win streak that ended in the 1975 state championship game, the Gobblers were 15-0-0 in 1973 scoring 477 points to 55 points; 15-0-0 in 1974 with 478 points to 66 points and 14-1-0 in 1975 with a 406-48 point difference. The 1994 Gobblers were 12-0-1 with 539 points to 93 points.

During the Doak Walker years, Highland Park went 12-1-0 in 1943 with the Scots scoring 476 to 76. In 1944, they were 11-2-1 putting up 420 points to 75 points. In 1945, they were 12-0-2 with a 468-56 margin as they won state. As they won state again in 1957, they were 11-1-1 with a 424-76 margin. In 1958, the Scots were 11-2 scoring 433 to 74 for their opponents. The 2005 team quarterbacked by Matthew Stafford scored 772 points as they won state.

Hondo in 1955 went 10-0-2 scoring 402 to 56 points. The 2006 Owl team was 14-1-0 and scored 666 points as it lost in the 3A -Div II Semi-Finals to state champion Liberty Hill.

Mart won State in 1969 with a 15-0-0 record and outscored the opposition 491-70. The 1999 State Champion Panther team led by Quan Cosby was 15-0-0 putting 789 points to 100 points. The Panthers averaged 52.6 points a game while giving up 6.67 points a game.

Plano had two teams put up offensive and defensive numbers of this magnitude, first in 1965 as the Wildcats were 14-1-0 scoring 418 points to 100 and then again in 1971 as they finished 13-1-0 with 454 points to 82 points. Those were both State Championship years for Plano.

Temple has six seasons with the 400-100 numbers. The Wildcats in 1921 were 10-1-0 with 426 points to 44 points. They had the same 10-1-0 record in 1933 scoring 415 points to 38 points. In 1951, they lost to Breckenridge High in the State Championship game going 11-2-0 and scoring 490 points to 72 points. In 1978, they were 11-1-0 with a 430 to 62 point differential. Coach Bob McQueen's team won state in 1979 with a 15-0-0 record and 480 points to 92 for their foes. The 1980 team played nearly as well going 11-1-0 and scoring 428 points to 80 points. The Tyler John Tyler Lions in 1938 were 12-0-1 with 401 points to 41 points.

STREAKS AND RECORDS-TEAM & INDIVIDUAL

Football is a sport where both teams and their individual members can set records. Streaks are normally thought of in football as being created and maintained by teams, especially since they can go on for years, far past the normal four year eligibility span for individual players. But individuals can set personal records on the field during their years at their school, some of which are certainly streaks. And they can be part of creating a long streak maintained by one school over many, many years. This chapter is created to give recognition to, first the records and streaks of the 12 teams featured in *Friday's Winners, and* then to the individual records set by the team members during the maximum four years they played for their respective teams. It is divided into two parts- team first and then individuals.

To start this off, I am presenting the records for the number of playoff games in which each team participated. You have heard the phrase," one and done", now used in today's sports language to describe the college careers of super star basketball players, who have to play one year of college basketball before being eligible to enter the draft for the NBA. Well, "one and done", has a lot to do with the top teams that are in this category. "One and done" in football playoff parlance at the high school level means that the team lost out in the Bi-District round, the first round of the playoffs. So the more times they can win playoff games to advance to the next level, the more they are achieving recognition as a top playoff team. A playoff appearance as shown at the top of each chapter is for each year they made it to at least Bi-District level. But if a team keeps winning, there can be as many as six games for it in one year's playoff appearance. The sixth game of course is playing for the State Championship.

That being said, here are the records for play- off game participation by each of the 12 teams in this book. The top school in total wins is Mart with 96 games under its belt. Next comes Highland Park with 89 wins. Plano is right on the Scots' heels with 88 wins. Cuero is next with 78 wins. Then comes Brownwood with 65 wins. Cameron Yoe has 58 wins followed by Amarillo with 56 wins. Longview is one behind the Sandies with 55 wins. Tyler John Tyler is next with 49 wins followed by Hondo with 48 victories. Tied with 46 wins each are Corsicana and Temple.

Most of these teams don't have as high a winning percentage in the playoffs as they do for all the games they have ever played. The competition gets tougher the further they advance in the playoffs, so a lower percentage is to be expected. Still a couple of teams stand out as the money teams to go with if you're a betting person. Cuero and Mart are almost neck and neck in winning playoff percentages with the Gobblers holding a slim .05 % margin over the Panthers. Cuero has won 72.98% of its 109 playoff games to 72.93% for Mart with 133 games. Plano is next with a 68.46% margin in 130 games. Brownwood follows with a 66.67% rate in 99 games. The Scots have won 63.35% of their 146 playoff games. Tyler John Tyler isn't too far behind at 62.269% in 79 games. The Yoemen of Cameron Yoe are next at 61.97% in 96 games.. Longview has won 59.68% of its 93 post regular season games. Amarillo barely nudges out Corsicana with a 54.24% in 106 games to the Tigers 54.11% in 85 games. Hondo has won 52.69% of its 93 playoff games. Temple is at a 50% rate in 98 games

Streaks are a fun category for fans of the various teams to talk and brag about. For the teams, the streaks can be for most consecutive wins in all games, most consecutive wins in district play and the most consecutive wins over certain opponents. Let's begin with consecutive winning seasons. Plano leads the way with 36 seasons between 1960 and 1995. Brownwood is next with 32 seasons between 1958 and 1989. Highland Park is on a current streak of 26 seasons between 1988 and 2013. Longview's win streak ran for 23 seasons between 1971 and 1993. Also having 23 season win streaks were Hondo from 1962 to 1984 and Amarillo from 1927 to 1949.

Leading the way in the most 10 win seasons is Highland Park-35, Mart-31, Plano-27, Brownwood and Cameron Yoe-22 each, Amarillo and Longview-21 each, Hondo-19 and Corsicana and Temple-17 each. The Scots also lead in the most undefeated regular seasons at 19. Amarillo is second with 16. Cameron Yoe trails the Sandies with 15. Temple has 13 undefeated regular season. Three schools tied at 11 seasons each are Corsicana, Hondo and Longview. Plano has 10 undefeated regular seasons.

Of course, points scored in a season is another measure of how well a team has done. With the gradual expansion to a season being either 15 or 16 games for teams playing for the State Championship and with the emergence of the spread offense causing big increases in the amounts of points scored in a game, the teams of the 21st century have put up some big numbers with Aledo going over 1000 points in 2013 setting the new mark. But nine of the 12 schools in the book have gotten their scoring for a season into the record books, some for several different years. Brownwood is tops with 801 points run up in 2010. Mart finished the equivalent of two touchdowns less than the Lions as they recorded 789 points in 1999. The Panthers also ran up 672 points in 2012 in 15 games. In 2013, they had 634 points in 14 games and again that many in 2000 in 16 games. In 2010, they played for 15 games and scored 625 points. Finally in 2004, they accumulated 602 points in 13 games.

Cameron Yoe in 2013 ran up 699 points in 16 games. In 2010, the Yoemen had 645 points in 15 games. Coming in with 695 points in 1987 was Cuero in 16 games. The Gobblers scored 660 points in 2007 in 15 games. They had 606 points in 2009 in 14 games. Hondo scored 666 points, the same number as their current total wins in 2006 in 15 games. Three years ago, Corsicana put up 656 points in 15 games. Tyler John Tyler has been among the top scoring leaders in two different seasons- 645 points in 2011 in 15 game and 635 points in 15 games in 2012. Temple had 613 points in 16 games in the state championship year of 1992. Highland Park shows up among the scoring leaders in 2009 with 644 points in 13 games, 2001 with 640 points in 14 games, 2013 with 629 points in 15 games and 2008 with 605 points in 13 games. Longview put together two high scoring years in a row as they went to the state finals in 2008 and 2009. The Lobos scored 612 and 602 points respectively.

What is somewhat strange is in contrast to most of the big scoring records for the total season taking place since 2000 is that virtually the scoring records for one game by one team took place in the earliest days of Texas high school football history, the 19 teens and the 1920s. But they didn't play as many games back then , so a team didn't have big end of the season totals as exists today. Anyway leading off the pack is Brownwood's annihilation of Goldwaithe with 132 points in 1928. Highland Park laid 128 points on Cooper in 1927. Temple got to Bartlett for 118 points in 1922. Amarillo ran up 113 points on Dalhart in 1913. Corsicana scored 115 points on Waxahachie in 1926. That same year Tyler put up 111 points on Palestine. In 1931, Amarillo put up 103 points on Woodard, OK. Tyler got 103 points on Mount Pleasant in 1927. Highland Park had 103 points on Grapevine in 1924. Amarillo blasted Quanah for 102 points in 1929. Plano blasted Wylie for 102 points in 1929. Amarillo scored 102 points on Hereford in 1921. Corsicana also scored 102 points on Ennis in 1915. Since 1950, Mart scored 90 points in 2003 against Bosqueville and 93 points over Itasca in 2014. Brownwood scored 88 points in a playoff game in 2010 against Iowa Park.

A part of streaks is long term series between two teams meeting year after year. Just looking at those series that have been a minimum of 75 years between the teams in this list and some of their opponents naturally shows that in most cases, our dozen teams have dominated each of the series. There are two series profiled that have gone over 100 meetings. The Cuero-Yoakum series has 104 games to date. It began in 1911. Cuero leads in the series 67-31-6. Longview and Marshall have met 103 times including 81 consecutive years. The Lobos lead the series 58-40-5.

Other series of note include Amarillo-Lubbock for 97 years including 89 consecutive years through 2012. The Sandies have won 38 meetings in a row and lead the series 81-14-2. Amarillo has played Pampa 85 times and leads that series 63-29-3. The Sandies have played Plainview 80 times and have a 59-21-4 lead over the Bulldogs. Cameron Yoe and Rockdale have met 84 teams. The Yoemen lead 58-24-2 in a series that began in 1913. Corsicana and Waxahachie have played each other 75 times with the Tigers on top 38-32-5.

Cuero has two other series of consequence, meaning at least 75 meetings, that started back as far as 1913. The Gobblers have met Edna 88 times and have a 53-30-5 advantage. They just opened the 2014 season meeting Gonzales in their 76th meeting. The Gobblers' win on September 5th moved their record between the two rivals to 39-36-1. Hondo has two other teams with long rivalries that they weren't playing in 2014. They lead Pearsall 64-29-7 in their series and they lead Uvalde 50-43-3 in that series. The Owls have met Devine 92 times and lead the series 57-33-2.

Mart played Groesbeck for 90 years, including a streak of 75 straight meetings. When the series ended, the Panthers had a 55-30-5 advantage. Longview has met fellow *Friday's Winners* profiler, Tyler John Tyler 87 times and lead the series 44-36-7. Tyler has met Marshall 85 times and leads the series 50-32-3.

This is a good representation of team records and streaks in which these 12 schools have had good participation. In the second part of this section are the records for individual players on these teams.

There aren't many players from these schools who are at the top of the all-time leaders in any one offensive category listed here. The one who stands out as being near the top is Robert Strait who played for the Cuero Gobblers from 1985 through 1988. He was a tough runner who finished as the number three all time rusher by the time he graduated. He ran for 8411 yards in those four years. Now he has slipped to number seven all-time as others have moved past him in the 25 years since he last suited up for the Gobblers. His name will show up in various ways in this chapter as we look at different milestones of achievement in carrying the ball.

Among other all time career leaders in rushing are Ketric Sanford of Corsicana with 6762 yards between 1993 and '95. The only other one on the career leaders list over 5000 yards is Tony Baker of Mart who gained 5333 yards between 1981 and 1984. In the schools in 5A ranks, Fred Talley of Longview ran for 4812 yards between 1996 and 1998. In Plano, Rex Burkhead ran for 4703 yards from 2006 through 2008. Lache Seastrunk of Temple zoomed for 4209 yards between 2007 and 2009. In the 4A ranks, Hut Allred of Brownwood gained 4667 yards between 1991 and 1993. Freddie Stoglin of Brownwood rushed for 4467 yards in 2000 through 2002.

Lamontra Owens of Corsicana was the leading rusher in single games as he ran for 457 yards against Sulphur Springs in 2013. Trent Jackson of Cuero picked up 385 yards on in 2010. Sanford of Corsicana gained 376 yards on Whitehouse in 1995. Trey Owens for Corsicana had 356 yards against Forney in 2012.

Season rushing leaders were paced by Strait with 3515 yards in 1987. Cameron Washington of Corsicana gained 3210 yards in 2011. Sanford had back to back high rushing seasons, 2761 in '94 and 2616 in '95. Jackson of Cuero picked up 2526 yards in 2009.

Strait carried the ball 1131 times in his four years, '85 through '88. Ketric Sanford made 1051 rushes for Corsicana in '93 through '95. Burkhead had 744 totes for the Plano Wildcats in 2006 to 2008. In individual seasons, Ketric led with 475 carries in 1994. Strait had 384 rushes in 1987. Washington of Corsicana carried the ball 352 times in 2011. Ketric had 330 rushes in 1995. In single game carries, Cody Evans of Corsicana had 44 carries in 2008 against Ennis. Owens of Corsicana carried 43 times against Sulphur Springs in 2013. Sanford carried 41 times in a game against Athens in 1993. Cameron Washington of Corsicana had 40 carries against Kilgore in 2011.

Current Detroit Lion quarterback Matthew Stafford was the career leading passer among these 12 schools as he led Highland Park with 8250 yards in 2003 through 2005. Jason Kopriva of Cameron Yoe wasn't too far behind with 8053 yards from 2011 through 2013. Tyler John Tyler's Greg Ward passed for 8018 yards from 2010 through 2012. Luke Woodley of Highland Park had 7941 yards between 2007 and 2009. Tyler Arndt passed for 7091 yards for Cuero between 2007 and 2009. Coming in with 6477 yards was Carson Meger of Plano from 2007 through 2008. Casey Pascall of Brownwood threw for 6355 yards in 2006 to 2008. Roddy Green of Mart passed for 5715 yards in 2003 to 2005. Brady Burgin of Highland Park picked up 5355 yards through the air in 2009 to 2011. Only four yards behind Burgin for his career with 5351 yards was Kyle Noack of Cuero from 2005 to 2006. Paul Johnson of Cameron Yoe passed for 4928 yards in 1985-1987. One who must have been considered a highly unusual quarterback when he set his passing records is Doyle Traylor of Temple who passed for 4899 yards way back in 1950 through 1952. Those kind of numbers rarely happened back then. Boy, is it ever different today.

Season leaders in passing began with Ward of Tyler throwing for 4202 yards in 2012. Woodley of Highland Park in 2009 threw for 4162 yards. Graylon Brown of Brownwood in 2010 threw for 4036 yards. Matthew Stafford of Highland Park tossed for 4013 yards in 2005. In 2011, Ward picked up 3784 yards through the air for the Lions. Woodley threw for 3746 yards in 2008. Jack Rhoades of Cameron Yoe passed for 3553 yards in 2010. Carson Meger of Plano got 3352 yards in 2007. The Scots' Brady Burgin gained 3313 yards overhead in 2011. Kopriva of Cameron Yoe passed for 3216 yards in 2012. Meger got the Wildcats 3135 yards in 2008.

Two passing leaders in individual games went over 500 yards. Ward passed for 552 yards against Denton Guyer in 2012. Woodley threw for 544 yards against Richardson Pearce in 2009. Just below 500 yard games were Ward with 494 yards against Pflugerville Hendrickson in 2011. Following him was Woodley with 479 yards completed against McKinney in 2009. That same year he had a 448 yard output against Rockwall. Chris Keesee of Brownwood torched Snyder for 415 yards in 2013. Stafford had two more games over 400 yards passing. In 2005 he threw for 404 yards against Terrell and in 2003, 403 yards against Ennis.

Stafford had 94 touchdown passes for the Scots from 2003 to 2005. Another Scot, Woodley followed with 81 scoring tosses in the 2007 to 2009 period. Ward pitched 78 for Tyler in his time there of 2010 through 2012. Arndt of Cuero connected for 75 scores from 2007 through 2009. The most outstanding passer for scores had to be Traylor of Temple who connected for 72 scores way back in the era of 1950-52, a time when scoring in this manner wasn't the in thing. With him at the helm, the Wildcats played for the State Championship in both 1951 and 1952, losing both times to Breckenridge.

Kopriva led in career completions with 618 over his three years. Ward had 566 completions. Woodley connected with his receivers 532 times. Stafford completed 511 passes. Arndt's targets caught 445 of his passes. Meger of Plano was five completions behind Arndt, but took only two years to reach that level, compared to three years for Arndt.

Ward's outstanding performance against Denton Guyer in 2012 in the State Semi-Finals made him the leader in most completions in one game with 48. Woodley completed 40 against Richardson Pearce in 2009. Zach Allen of Temple hit 35 completions over South Lake Carroll in 2012. Keesee made 31 passes against Graham in 2013 and followed with 29 completions that same year over Fort Worth All Saints. Also connecting on 29 completions were Ward against Corsicana in 2012 and Woodley against Waco Midway in 2008.

Streaks and Records-team & Individual

The passers had to have someone to throw to in order to compile those long distance yards. Here are the career receivers in the dozen schools. Fred Ross of Tyler grabbed 208 between 2010-2012. Kris Lott of Plano had 149 catches in 2007-08. Tre Gray of Cuero snatched 145 from 2004 through 2006. Darion Flowers of Tyler made 133 catches in the two years 2011-12. William Moore of Highland Park grabbed 128 passes in 2011-12 as did Derek Stanford of Temple from 1994 to 1996. Cameron Yoe's Derek Evans snatched 124 tosses in 2004-05. Another Yoe player, Aaron Sims took in 122 passes in 2011 through 2013. Jon Bauer of Corsicana caught 120 passes in 2003-04. Robert Armstrong of Cuero grabbed 117 passes in the two year period 2007-08.

The one season leaders began with Ross making 99 catches in 2011. Lott of Plano made 81 catches in 2008. Morris of Highland Park grabbed 80 catches in 2011. Conner Howard of Brownwood made 76 catches last season in 2013. Seth Gardener of Highland Park grabbed 73 catches in 2007. Sims of Cameron Yoe caught 71 passes in 2013. Adam Parsons of Highland Park took in 70 receptions from presumably Stafford in 2003.

The final category for receivers is touchdown catches. For a career, it's Ross of Tyler with 39 from 2010 through 2012. Omarious Hines of Corsicana caught 36 from 2006 through 2009. Damian Davis of Mart scored on 33 pass receptions from 2005 and 2006. Season leaders are Jaxon Shipley of Brownwood with 27 TDs in 2010. Ross of Tyler managed 22 scoring plays in 2012. Gardener of Highland Park caught 21 scoring passes in 2007. Chris Hipps of Highland Park had 17 catches in 2009. Davis of Mart matched that performance in 2005 as did Adam Parsons of Highland Park in 2003. Two players each caught 16 touchdown passes-Dalton Stogner of Highland Park in 2010 and Davis of Mart in 2006.

Some players made their way into the record books with their feet. Dillon Ellis kicked 98 extra points for Brownwood in 2010. Adam Deike booted 86 for Mart as it won the state championship in 1999. Jonathan Perez of Cuero kicked 81 EPs in 2007. In 2013, Will Sanders of Highland Park connected through the uprights 77 times. Martin Rodriquez of Cameron Yoe was one behind with 76 successful PATs in 2010. It's an old Sandie who is in the record books as an extra points leader in one game. Windy Nicklaus of Amarillo split the uprights 12 times against Hereford in 1921.

Finally we come to career scoring and Robert Strait's name pops up again. He is fifth all time in career points scored with 841 points between 1985 and 1988. He is also fifth in career touchdowns with 128 for those years. He had 54 touchdowns in 1987. He is fourth all time for the most points in a single season with 372 points in 1987. He also had 337 points in 1986. In 2011, Cameron Washington scored 276 points for Corsicana on 46 touchdowns.

Strait had a game in 1987 against Smithville in which he had seven touchdowns and 47 points. D'Narian Thomas of Mart matched him on touchdowns in one game with seven against Alto in 2012, good for 42 points.

While none of the players in this chapter were the absolute all-time leader in any category, they were among the leaders which is reflected in the contribution each of them made to their teams to help them be a part of *Friday's Winners*.

CHANGES, BUT NO SURPRISES

Remember in the first chapter in *Friday's Winners, About Friday's Winners,* I dedicated this book to Joe Lee Smith, the man who has spent over half a century doing the research on Texas high school football teams? I mentioned then that he continues to do this research almost on a daily basis. That is because there are new facts turning up constantly about games played long ago, reports that had erroneous information just now being corrected on scores, names of coaches and won-loss records. He pays to rent archive data bases from newspapers to aid him in searching for the correct information. He relies on people like me and coaches who have knowledge to inform him of facts that need to be changed or added to his data base.

So it came as no surprise to me that I received an e mail from him on August 2, 2014 telling me of some more wins that he found for three of the schools profiled in *Friday's Winners. I thought I would emphasize his work by listing his new information adding wins to schools in my book in this final chapter. His new studies came up with changes in won-loss records for 120 schools. So with no further ado, here are the changes for Amarillo High, Plano Senior High and Temple High. While it added to their totals, it didn't change their standings in the order of where they are among the dozen schools I've written about. Plano had the biggest increase in new wins, four, but also Joe Lee found three more losses to add to its all-time records.*

Plano-October 29, 1906-lost to Mesquite HS 3-0
November 4, 1909-beat the Plano Town Team 5-0
1911-beat the Richardson City Team 6-0
October 31, 1913-beat the Mesquite Town Team 26-0
November 14, 1914-lost to West Dallas HS 6-3
September 28. 1917-lost to Rockwall 7-0
Temple-November 4, 1905-beat Belton 27-0
December 26, 1905-beat Fullvia Academy of Temple 5-0
Amarillo-November 29, 1909-beat Hereford College, a forerunner of Hereford HS 15-0

So if you go to Joe Lee Smith's data base, the section devoted to the most wins will show Amarillo second with 744 wins, Plano third with 738 wins and Temple fourth with 712 wins. Of course, these new win totals should be on the front page of each chapter on these schools, but I wanted you to see how information is constantly changing. Perhaps you might have some old newspapers stored away in the attic that would provide information to increase the wins of your favorite team and perhaps in the process, knock a hated rival down in the ranks.

UPDATE ON 2014 GAMES

It took me longer to finish *Friday's Winners* than I anticipated. Seven weeks of the 2014 regular season games have gone by as of publishing time. Here are those scores of the 12 teams plus those of the two schools within eight games of being in the bottom rungs of wins accumulated by the dozen teams.

AMARILLO	8-28-14-W Palo Duro 45-21; 9-5-14-Wichita Falls Rider W 35-20; 9-12-14 EP Montwood W 51-20;9-19-14 W Odessa 27-0; 9-26-14- W Midland-21-10; 10-3-14 W Abilene Cooper 28-17; 10-10-14 W Lubbock Coronado 56-10
BROWNWOOD	8-28-14 W Gatesville 35-0; 9-5-14 L Graham 15-40; 9-12-14 L Liberty Hill L 36-43; 9-19-14 W Alvarado 29-15; 9-26-14 W-Burkburnett-37-8; 10-3-14 W FW Springtown 30-7; 10-10-14 L Stephenville 40-21;
CAMERON YOE	8-28-14-L Waco Connally-49-63; 9-5-14-W Lexington 47-13; 9-12-14 L China Spring 14-23 9-19-14-W Whitney-47-27; 9-26-14 L Refugio 7-19; 10-10-14 L Rockdale 34-27;
CORSICANA	8-29-14 L Northwest 14-34; 9-5-14 L The Colony-15-22; 9-12-14 W Granbury 25-10' 9-26-14 W Lindale 24-23; 10-3-14 W Jacksonville 30-14;10-10-14 L Nacogdoches 49-21
CUERO	8-29-14 W Wharton 37-20; 9-5-14 W Gonzales 35-0; 9-12-14 W Smithville 38-0; 9-19-14 L Calhoun 17-21; 9-26-14 W Columbus 28-20; 10-3-14 W Giddings 35-24; 10-10-14 W Yoakum 44-34;
HIGHLAND PARK	8-30-14 Centennial 47-0; 9-5-14 W Pulaski Academy 48-42; 9-12-14 W Prosper 54-0; 9-26-14 W North

Friday's Winners

	Mesquite 29-9; 10-3-14 W Richardson Pearce 56-0; 10-10-14 L Mesquite Horn 42-27
HONDO	8-29-14 L Boerne 22-38; 9-5-14 W Jourdanton 20-14; 9-12-14 W Medina Valley 27-21; 9 -19-14 L Holy Cross 0-20; 9-26-14 L Devine 23-28; 10-3-14 W Carrizo Springs 37-0
LONGVIEW	9-29-14 L Lufkin 14-44; 9-5-14 L Tyler John Tyler L 25-41; 9-19-26 W Neville 19-13; 9-26-14 W Longview Pine Tree 66-13; 10-3-14 W Greenville 56-7; W Marshall 56-7;
MART	8-28-14 W Goldwaithe 41-14; 9-5-14 W Normangee 60-8; 9-12-14 W McGregor W 54-23; 9-19-14 W Thorndale 35-14; 9-26-14 W Centerville 49-28; 10-10-14 W Itasca 93-6;
PLANO	8-28-14 L Tyler John Tyler 12-30; 9-5-14 W McArthur 34-20; 9-12-14 W Hebron 35-14; 9-18-14 L Allen 3-42; 9-26-14 W Flower Mound 35-13; 10-3-14 W Plano West 17-14; 10-10-14 W Plano East 34-6
TEMPLE	8-29-14 W Round Rock 35-28; 9-5-14 L Austin Westlake 48-49; 9-19-14 W Harker Heights 59-14 9-26-14 W Waco University 70-0; 10-3-14 W Manor 28-14 10-10-14 Pflugerville Connally W 63-7;
TYLER JOHN TYLER	8-28-14 W Plano 30-12; 9-5-14- W Longview 41-25; 9-12-14 L Tyler Lee 31-37; 9-26-14 W Whitehouse 52-37; 10-3-14 W Lindale 76-13;W Lufkin 25-24;

THE TWO SCHOOLS CLOSEST TO THE FRIDAY'S WINNERS GROUP IN WINS TO BEGIN 2014

REFUGIO	8-29-14 W Hebronville 54-0; 9-5-14 W Mathis 56-13; 9-19-14 W San Diego 40-0; 9-26-14 W Cameron Yoe 19-7; 10-3-14 W Banquette; 10-10-14 W Shiner 34-28;
ABILENE	8-29-14 W Heritage 38-17; 9-5-14 W Warren 38-7; 9-12-14 W Cooper 38-7; 9-19-14 W LD Bell 38-12; 9-26-14 L Southlake Carroll 21-56; 10-10-14-L San Angelo Central 21-20

Made in the USA
Columbia, SC
14 November 2020